FREEDOM TO RO

I0642732

Forest of Bowland

WITH PENDLE HILL AND
THE WEST PENNINE MOORS

Forest of Bowland

WITH PENDLE HILL
AND THE WEST PENNINE MOORS

Andrew Bibby

FRANCES LINCOLN

The Freedom to Roam guides
are dedicated to the memory of
Benny Rothman

Frances Lincoln Ltd, 4 Torriano Mews, Torriano Avenue, London NW5 2RZ,
www.franceslincoln.com

Forest of Bowland
Copyright © Andrew Bibby 2005

All photographs except those on pages 69, 76–7, 81, 92, 126–7, 130–1, 137, 145, 150–1
by Charlie Hedley © Countryside Agency
Photographs pages 69, 76–7, 126–7, 145, 150–1 © Andrew Bibby; photograph page 81
© John Howard; photograph page 92 by Laurie Campbell © rspb-images.com;
photograph pages 130–1 © Chris Clegg; photograph page 137 © John Morrison;
illustration page 160 © Martin Bagness

Lyrics from 'The Manchester Rambler' song by Ewan MacColl used by kind permission of
Peggy Seeger and of the publisher Harmony Music Ltd

Maps reproduced from Ordnance Survey mapping on behalf of The Controller
of Her Majesty's Stationery Office © Crown Copyright 100043293 2004

First published by Frances Lincoln 2005

The right of Andrew Bibby to be identified as the author of this work has been asserted
by him in accordance with the Copyright, Design and Patents Act 1988 (UK)

British Library Cataloguing in Publication Data
A catalogue record for this book is available from the British Library

ISBN 0-7112-2502-8
Printed and bound in Singapore by Kyodo Printing Co.
9 8 7 6 5 4 3 2 1

Frontispiece photograph: Trough of Bowland

Contents

Acknowledgments 6
Series introduction 7
Walking in open country – a guide to using this book 9
Introduction 16
1   Ward's Stone and High Stephen's Head 24
    Feature: Bowland's bogs 32
2   Harrisend Fell 34
    Feature: Sorry, I haven't a clough 37
3   Hawthornthwaite 39
    Feature: Getting ready for access 44
4   Bleasdale and Fair Snape 47
    Feature: Managing the moors 55
5   Bleadale Water 59
    Feature: The centre of the kingdom 67
6   Wolfhole Crag 70
    Feature: The Romans in Bowland 78
7   Whitendale and the Roman Road 83
    Feature: Hen harriers 91
    Feature: Slaidburn 94
8   Roeburndale 95
    Feature: Raven Castle 101
9   Raven's Castle 105
    Feature: A vision on Pendle Hill 111
10 Robin Hood's Well (Pendle Hill) 113
11 Pendle Hill Big End 121
    Feature: The Clarion House 129
12 Darwen Moor 133
13 Round Loaf (Anglezarke Moor) 139
    Feature: The battle for Winter Hill 144
14 Winter Hill 147
Some further reading 155
The Country Code 157
Index 158
Area map of the walk routes 160

Acknowledgments

The author gratefully acknowledges the assistance given him by a wide range of individuals and organizations, and is particularly grateful for the help offered by Tarja Wilson of Lancashire County Council, David Kelly, Gwen Goddard, Kate Conto and Dan French of the Ramblers' Association, and Kate Cave and Fiona Robertson at Frances Lincoln. Also much appreciated has been the assistance offered by Peter Wilson (RSPB), Nick Osborne, Don McKay and Susan Conway (Lancashire County Council), Peter Iles (Lancashire County Archaeological Service), Jon Hickling (English Nature), Liane Bradbrook (Countryside Agency), Rod Banks (Abbeystead Estate), Jeremy Duckworth (Bleasdale estate), Carl Oysten, John Howard, Clive Upton (University of Leeds), Derek Stanton and Peter Wright (Lancashire Dialect Society), John Cowking (Slaidburn Silver Band), Carol Hopkins, Charlie Hedley, Jonathan Ratter, Philip Hudson, Richard Peters, Richard Leonard, Jane Smith, Maureen Wagner, Harry Seccombe, Catherine Putz, Mark Holtom and Jane Scullion.

Series introduction

This book, and the companion books in the series, celebrate the arrival in England and Wales of the legal right to walk in open country. The title for the series is borrowed from a phrase much used during the long campaign for this right – Freedom to Roam. For years, it was the dream of many to be able to walk at will across mountain top, moorland and heath, free of the risk of being confronted by a 'Keep Out' sign or being turned back by a gamekeeper.

The sense of frustration that the hills were, in many cases, out of bounds to ordinary people was captured in the song 'The Manchester Rambler' written by one of the best-known figures in Britain's post-war folk revival, Ewan MacColl. The song, which was inspired by the 1932 'mass trespass' on Kinder Scout when walkers from Sheffield and Manchester took to the forbidden Peak District hills, tells the tale of an encounter between a walker, trespassing on open land, and an irate gamekeeper:

He called me a louse, and said 'Think of the grouse',
Well I thought but I still couldn't see
Why old Kinder Scout, and the moors round about
Couldn't take both the poor grouse and me.

The desire, as Ewan MacColl expressed it, was a simple one:

So I'll walk where I will, over mountain and hill
And I'll lie where the bracken is deep,
I belong to the mountains, the clear running fountains
Where the grey rocks rise ragged and steep.

Some who loved the outdoors and campaigned around the time of the Kinder Scout trespass in the 1930s must have thought that the legal right to walk in open country would be won after the Second World War, at the time when the National Parks were being created and the rights-of-way network drawn up. It was not to be. It was another half century before, finally, Parliament passed the Countryside and Rights of Way Act 2000, and the people of England and Wales gained the legal right to take to the hills and the moors. (Scotland has its own traditions and its own legislation.)

We have dedicated this series to the memory of Benny Rothman, one of the leaders of the 1932 Kinder Scout mass trespass who was imprisoned for his part in what was deemed a 'riotous assembly'. Later in his life, Benny Rothman was a familiar figure at rallies called by the Ramblers' Association as once again the issue of access rights came to the fore. But we should pay tribute to all who have campaigned for this goal. Securing greater access to the countryside was one of the principles on which the Ramblers' Association was founded in 1935, and for many ramblers the access legislation represents the achievement of literally a lifetime of campaigning.

So now, at last, we do have freedom to roam. For the first time in several centuries, the open mountains, moors and heaths of England and Wales are legally open for all. We have the protected right to get our boots wet in the peat bogs, to flounder in the tussocks, to blunder and scrabble through the bracken and heather, and to discover countryside which, legally, we had no way of knowing before.

The Freedom to Roam series of books has one aim: to encourage you to explore and grow to love these new areas of the countryside which are now open to us. The right to roam freely – that's surely something to celebrate.

Walking in open country – a guide to using this book

If the right and the freedom to roam openly are so important – perceptive readers may be asking – why produce a set of books to tell you where to go?

So a word of explanation about this series. The aim is certainly not to encourage walkers to follow each other ant-like over the hills, sticking rigidly to a pre-determined itinerary. We are not trying to be prescriptive, instructing you on your walk stile by stile or gate by gate. The books are not meant as instruction manuals but we hope that they will be valuable as *guides* – helping you discover areas of the countryside which you haven't legally walked on before, advising you on routes you might want to take, and telling you about places of interest on the way.

In areas where it can be tricky to find routes or track down landmarks, we offer more detailed instructions.

Elsewhere, we are deliberately less precise in our directions, allowing you to choose your own path or line to follow. For each walk, however, there is a recommended core route, and this forms the basis on which the distances given are calculated.

There is, then, an assumption that those who use this book will be comfortable with using a map – and that, in practice, means one of the Ordnance Survey's 1:25 000 Explorer series of maps. As well as referring to the maps in this book, it is worth taking the full OS map with you, to give you a wider picture of the countryside you will be exploring.

Safety in the hills

Those who already are experienced upland walkers will not be surprised if at this point we put in a note on basic safety in the hills. Walkers need to remember that walking in open country, particularly high country, is different from footpath walking across farmland or more gentle countryside. The main risk is of being inadequately prepared for changes in the weather. Even in high summer, hail and snow are not impossible. Daniel Defoe found this out in August 1724 when he crossed the Pennines from Rochdale, leaving a calm clear day behind to find himself almost lost in a blizzard on the tops.

If rain comes, the temperature will drop, so it is important to be properly equipped and to guard against hypothermia. Fortunately, walkers today have access to a range of wind- and rain-proof clothing which was not available in the eighteenth century. Conversely, in hot weather, take sufficient water to avoid the risk of dehydration and hyperthermia (dangerous

overheating of the body).

Be prepared for visibility to drop, when (to use the local term) the clag descends on the hills. It is always sensible to take a compass. If you are unfamiliar with basic compass-and-map work, ask in a local outdoor equipment shop whether they have simple guides available or pick the brains of a more experienced walker.

The other main hazard, even for walkers who know the hills well, is that of suffering an accident such as a broken limb. If you plan to walk alone, it is sensible to tell someone in advance where you will be walking and when you expect to be back – the moorland and mountain rescue services which operate in the areas covered by this book are very experienced but they are not psychic. Groups of walkers should tackle only what the least experienced or least fit member of the party can comfortably achieve. Take particular care if you intend to take children with you to hill country. And take a mobile phone by all means, but don't assume you can rely on it, since some parts of the moors and hills will not pick up a signal. (If you can make a call and are in a real emergency situation, ring 999 – it is the police who coordinate mountain and moorland rescues.)

If this sounds off-putting, that is certainly not the intention. The guiding principle behind the access legislation is that walkers will exercise their new-won rights with responsibility. Taking appropriate safety precautions is simply one aspect of acting responsibly.

Access land – what you can and can't do

The countryside which is covered by access legislation includes mountain, moor, heath, downland and common land. After the passing of the Countryside and Rights of Way Act 2000, a lengthy mapping process was undertaken, culminating in the production of 'conclusive' maps which identify land which is open for access. These maps (although not intended as guides for walking) can be accessed via the Internet, at www.countrysideaccess.gov.uk. Ordnance Survey maps

Note Each walk has been graded, on a scale of 🥾 to 🥾 🥾 🥾 🥾 🥾, for the degree of difficulty involved. In general, walks are judged more difficult if they are (a) longer in mileage, and/or (b) involve more rough walking (across open moorland rather than on established footpaths), and/or (c) pose more navigational problems or venture into very unfrequented areas. But bear in mind that all the walks in this book require map-reading competence and some experience of hill walking.

published from 2004 onwards also show access land.

You can walk, run, birdwatch and climb on access land, although there is no new right to camp or to bathe in streams or lakes (or, of course, to drive vehicles). The regulations sensibly insist that dogs, where permitted, are on leads near livestock and during the bird nesting season (1 March to 31 July). However grouse moors have the right to ban dogs altogether, and in most of the Forest of Bowland area (though not Pendle or the West Pennine Moors) this is what is happening. For more

information, watch out for local signs.

Access legislation also does not include the right to ride horses or bikes, though in some areas there may be pre-existing agreements which allow this. More information is available on the website given above and, at the time of writing, there is also an advice line on 0845 100 3298.

The access legislation allows for some open country to be permanently excluded from the right to roam. 'Excepted' land includes military land, quarries and areas close to buildings; in addition landowners can apply

On Pendle Hill

for other open land to be excluded. For example, at the time of writing, a number of areas of moorland used as rifle ranges have been designated in this way (these are not in areas covered by walks in this book).

To the best of the authors' knowledge, all the walks in the Freedom to Roam series are either on legal rights of way or across access land included in the official 'conclusive' maps. However, bear in mind that the books have been produced right at the start of the new access arrangements, before walkers have begun regularly to walk the hills and before any problems have been ironed out. For instance, at the time of writing there were still some places where entry to access land had not been finalized. As access becomes better established, it may be that minor changes to the routes suggested in these books will become appropriate or necessary. You are asked to remember that we are encouraging you to be flexible in the way you use these guides.

Walkers in open country also need to be aware that landowners have a further right to suspend or restrict access on their land for up to twenty-eight days a year. (In such cases of temporary closure, there will normally be access on public holidays and most weekends.) Notice needs to be given in advance, and the plan is that this information should be readily available, it is hoped at local information centres and libraries but also on the countryside access website and at popular entry points to access land. This sort of set-up has generally worked well in Scotland, where walkers in areas where deer hunting takes place have been able to find out when and where hunting is happening.

Walkers will understand the sense in briefly closing small areas of open country when, for example, shooting is in progress (grouse shooting begins on 12 August) or when heather burning is taking place in spring. However, it is once again too early in the implementation of the access legislation to know how easily walkers in England and Wales will be able to find out about these temporary access closures. It is also too early to know whether landowners will attempt to abuse this power.

In some circumstances, additional restrictions on access can be introduced – for example, on the grounds of nature conservation or heritage conservation, on the advice of English Nature and English Heritage.

Bear these points in mind, but enjoy your walking in the knowledge that any access restrictions should be the exception and not the norm. The Countryside Agency has itself stated that 'restrictions will be kept to a minimum'. If you find access unexpectedly denied while walking in the areas suggested in this book, please accept the restrictions and follow the advice you are given. However, if you feel that access was wrongly denied, please report your

experience to the countryside service of the local authority (or National Park authority, in National Park areas), and to the Ramblers' Association.

Finally, you may sometimes choose not to exercise your freedom to roam. Many of the upland moors featured in these books are the homes of ground-nesting birds such as grouse, curlew, lapwing and pipit, who build their nests in spring and early summer. During this time, many people will decide to leave the birds in peace and find other places to walk. Rest assured you will know if you are approaching an important nesting area – birds are good at telling you that they would like you to go away.

Celebrating the open countryside

Despite these necessary caveats, the message from this series is, we hope, clear. Make the most of the new legal rights we have been given – and enjoy your walking.

Introduction

'A place of beauty and breezes, with moors above and pleasant foothills below'. This was how the *Guardian* – or as it was then the *Manchester Guardian* – described the Forest of Bowland area, in a feature which appeared in the paper back in February 1930. It was a delightful stretch of countryside but also, the *Manchester Guardian* had to admit, a place 'familiar only to the discerning few'.

The article was reporting on a forthcoming meeting in Manchester, which was set to discuss the possibility of arranging for the Forest of Bowland to be designated as a National Park. As the paper pointed out, the Lake District or the Peak District or Snowdonia might perhaps come to mind more readily as contenders for National Park status, but Bowland's considerable charms also made it a strong candidate: 'Fells that have most picturesque names are tumbled in delightfully natural disorder over thousands of acres that yield little but sparse grazing for mountain sheep. The very carelessness and profusion with which Nature has thrown these hills together is the characteristic feature of the greater part of the country.' Wild moors, wooded valleys – and Manchester only thirty miles away.

The Lake District, the Peak District, Snowdonia and many other beautiful areas of Britain did indeed go on to become National Parks, though two decades and a world war had to be lived through in the interim. But the meeting in Manchester in 1930 was not productive: it was not until 1964 that Bowland, together with the countryside around Pendle Hill, received official designation and then not as a National Park but rather one step down, as an Area of Outstanding Natural Beauty.

There are many within Bowland who would see this as a very satisfactory result. Bowland has avoided the pressures which have come, in some National Parks, from large numbers of visitors, and perhaps as a consequence the Bowland moorlands remain an extremely important natural habitat (this is the only part of England where, for example, the hen harrier regularly breeds). As in 1930, the area remains little known, even within Lancashire and the north-west: those moors described so vividly by the *Manchester Guardian* are still only 'familiar to the discerning few'.

But, and here we enter a potentially contentious area, one reason so few visitors have discovered the delights of Bowland's fells for themselves is that they haven't been encouraged to do so. In fact, until very recently, in many places they weren't legally allowed to: there were 'Private' signs out in force at the entrance points to large swathes of the upland moors. Bowland is a place where shooting matters a great deal, and where as a consequence grouse matter a great deal. Why, if you happened to be a landowner with many thousands of acres of grouse moors, would you have wanted to complicate things unnecessarily by allowing the public to share the moors with your grouse?

It was not only the 'Keep Out' signs which kept the public away. Landowners could and did use their powers to ensure that facilities for visitors did not develop: for example, tenant farmers could be restricted, under the terms of their leases, from taking in B&B guests or opening up tea rooms.

It is to a large extent because of the power of the large shooting estates that Bowland still has a private feel to it – it is the sort of area which can seem hard to get to know, where visitors can feel they are intruding into someone else's environment and someone else's way of life. Bowland can sometimes feel a long way from modern, urban, multicultural, twenty-first-century England. Here the sport that matters takes place not with a football but with a gun; 12 August, the start of the grouse shooting season, is the key date in the calendar.

'Feudal' is too simplistic a word to use to describe relationships here – but perhaps only just.

And so, because of all this, Bowland took on something of a symbolic status for ramblers during the many long years when the campaign for the right to roam was being waged. Bowland was the example held up above all others of beautiful moorland where the public was told, brutally, 'Keep Out'. Bowland was the great, elusive prize for which access rights

were being demanded. And Bowland was the place where many of the most significant access demonstrations during the 1990s were held – including rallies held in such unlikely windswept, remote and boggy places as Brennand Great Hill and White Hill.

It certainly didn't hurt the access campaign that the largest private landowner in the Forest of Bowland, latterly with over 23,000 acres in the estate, happened to be one of Britain's

Wolfhole Crag

richest men: the Duke of Westminster. His Grace, and his guests, had the opportunity to enjoy the Bowland moors, guns in hand. Why not, campaigners asked, the rest of us?

(Actually, it is not strictly correct to say that the current Duke of Westminster owns much of Bowland. Abbeystead House and the shooting estate which comes with it is owned by a family trust set up back in the 1960s to avoid hefty capital transfer tax liabilities. The duke himself rents the house and shooting rights back from this family trust. But perhaps this merely strengthens the argument.)

Public access to open country has now, of course, arrived in Bowland, an event which this book is in part here to commemorate. But there remains potentially a major cultural gap between visiting walkers and those who work for the big estates. The scope for mutual misunderstanding is considerable. For many of us, the idea that the apogee of some people's year is to stand at a grouse butt shooting at moorland birds as they flap by overhead seems incomprehensible. Why do it? Why go to so much trouble cosseting the grouse in the first place, just so that they can be shot later?

On the other hand, those who live and work close to the moors express irritation at the worst excesses of the 'anorak brigade'. (Not many walkers wear anoraks these days, but never mind, the term is still used.) There is, they suggest, a lack of comprehension on the part of the public of the work which goes on month by month to manage the moors, which helps to maintain their beauty and their importance as a natural habitat. Encouraging grouse shooting actually helps conservation (the argument may sound counterintuitive to the town-dweller, but it is one which is held with great passion).

While this book clearly takes a pro-access stance, perhaps its publication can help to move us beyond some of the old entrenched positions of the past. Walkers who really want to enjoy Bowland will want to understand what goes on in these hills, and that means understanding the work undertaken on the big shooting estates. For this reason, one section of this book will look in detail at the work which the Abbeystead estate carries out in managing its grouse moors.

It's also appropriate to recall that Bowland was never entirely out of bounds. In the 1990s, North West Water (now United Utilities) adopted an enlightened policy on access to its vast 26,000-acre moorland estate, with a presumption towards access. As North West Water put it at the time, 'The company's wildlife wardens and tenants' gamekeepers will not prevent suitably equipped walkers from choosing their own route, unless there is a reason why a particular area is temporarily closed, for example on shooting days or during the nesting season.' Abbeystead estate too had some experience of public access, through the Clougha access area agreement which it first signed with Lancashire County Council in 1972, later extended to an additional access area near White Moor.

It may not be coincidental that today much of the activity on the Bowland fells is dedicated to grouse shooting, given the area's history as a medieval hunting reserve. One question sometimes asked by first-time visitors exploring the high Bowland fells is: where is the forest? While in earlier times the moors would certainly have had more trees (early clearances, followed by over-grazing by sheep mean that the uplands are now lacking much tree cover), the question misses the point. Bowland was a forest in the same way as the New Forest and, closer to hand, the Forest of Pendle and the Forest of Rossendale were forests: in other words, they were stretches of countryside put aside for royal hunting.

In the part of upland Bowland which was historically in Yorkshire (roughly, the land east of the main watershed), the area's status as a royal forest continued until 1662. A smaller area in the historical jurisdiction of Lancashire ('Little Bolland') was a forest until 1556, and other parts of what is now

...erically the Forest of Bowland area were also separate ...unting estates. In each case forest laws applied with exacting penalties for any who poached. Forest courts were held in a number of places, including what are now the Inn at Whitewell and the Hark to Bounty pub in Slaidburn.

Managing the Forest was, in fact, not entirely dissimilar from managing today's grouse estates. In overall charge was the master forester, generally a member of the nobility or local gentry, who was granted his office by the king. The master forester would delegate the work to teams of foresters, whose chief task was to protect the deer. The foresters also protected the timber, took rents from tenants who had a right to graze livestock within the forest perimeters, checked that pannage (the right to allow pigs to scavenge for such things as acorns) was not being abused and impounded animals which were in the forest area illegally.

Though several centuries have passed since then, some people may want to trace back to the Forest days some of the attributes and atmosphere of Bowland today. This argument should be advanced cautiously, however: Bowland's moors also saw their fair share of industrial activity in the eighteenth and nineteenth centuries. Lead ore was mined and smelted near Brennand, for example, while the north of Bowland near Goodber Common and the west near Quernmore were important coal-mining areas. These industries have disappeared today, but if you know where to look you can see that they have left their mark on the Bowland landscape.

This book focuses particularly on Bowland because of its role and symbolism in the campaign for open access. Two walks, however, are included from another former hunting area, the Forest of Pendle, separated from Bowland geographically by the Ribble valley but linked to it geologically (in both areas Pennine gritstone is the dominant rock) and to an extent administratively, since Pendle is part of the overall

Bowland Area of Outstanding Natural Beauty. Pendle is a deservedly popular place with walkers, who have long had the opportunity to roam at will across this great whale of a hill.

Finally, three walks are included from the West Pennine Moors, another area offering wonderful moorland walking where, in most places, open access has been possible for many years. (As this book will recount, the right to walk some of these moors was gained more than a century ago, though not always without a struggle.) The west Pennines have been an outdoor playground for generations from the urban areas of south and central Lancashire, from places such as Bolton, Bury, Blackburn and Accrington. Three walks hardly do justice to this interesting area, but perhaps they will at least whet some readers' appetites.

WALK 1

WARD'S STONE AND
HIGH STEPHEN'S HEAD

DIFFICULTY 🥾 🥾 🥾 🥾 **DISTANCE 10½ miles (17 km)**

| LITTLE CRAGG (LITTLEDALE) | CLOUGHA | WARD'S STONE | HIGH STEPHEN'S HEAD | HAYLOT FELL | DEEP CLOUGH | LITTLE CRAGG |

MAP OS Explorer OL41, Forest of Bowland

STARTING POINT Little Cragg (GR 548618)

PARKING Parking is possible at Little Cragg, on Littledale Road (parking shown on OS maps).

PUBLIC TRANSPORT Unfortunately no buses pass near by. The nearest bus stops are in Brookhouse (services from Lancaster, Ingleton and Kirkby Lonsdale), about 2 miles (3 km) to the north.

This is one of the classic Bowland high-level routes, making use of the established route between Clougha and Ward's Stone. The return route is across land previously inaccessible to the public. Wet and boggy sections, with some rough walking.

▶ Take the footpath past Skelbow Barn **❶**, and turn right up the side of Sweet Beck to reach the open moors. Here a relatively well-walked footpath can be found, climbing steadily ahead up the hillside. Near the top, cross the shooting road and continue to the brow.

At this point, you may want briefly to turn right, to stroll to the nearby cairn ❷. The trig point at Clougha Pike itself lies a few minutes' walk further west.

■ Clougha Pike and the moors which surround it were the subject of one of the first formal access agreements, made in 1972 between Lancashire County Council and the Abbeystead estate. The agreement has meant that Clougha (pronounced 'cloffa') has, up to now, been one of the best-explored fells in Bowland.

Weather permitting, the view from here includes the vista across Morecambe Bay towards the Lakeland fells. Rather closer at hand, and perhaps less attractive, is the nuclear power station at Heysham.

▶ From the brow, take the ridge path heading eastwards, initially towards Grit Fell. At a number of points the path skirts areas of blanket bog and can be wet.

Continue for well over a mile (1.6 km), crossing a second time the estate shooting road which has been constructed over the hill. The next target, Ward's Stone, lies ahead ❸.

■ Ward's Stone is the highest point in the Forest of Bowland, at 1840 ft (561 m). In good weather, there is a panoramic view to enjoy, particularly north to the Three Peaks, the Howgill fells and the Lake District mountains.

The summit is, in fact, a plateau which has been given *two* OS trig points, one at the eastern end and one at the western end. The difference in height between them is only 3 ft (1 m) and – assuming you haven't first consulted the map – you may want to try to guess which one is the higher of the two. Somehow the answer seems surprising.

Ward's Stone itself is the rocky outcrop at the west of the plateau. The OS maps give the name Grey Mare and Foal to the outcrop at the eastern end. Another rock marked on maps, the Queen's Chair ❹, is a small circular rock near by – more a stool than a chair.

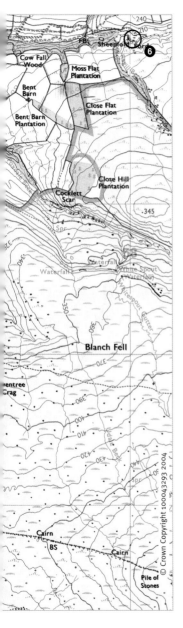

▶ From the eastern end of the Ward's Stone plateau a fence runs off diagonally towards the next destination, High Stephen's Head. Be warned that following this fence involves coping with some seriously wet areas of bog. A better strategy is to continue along the main path (with another fence to your left) for about ½ mile (0.8 km).

■ At this point, the walk approaches close to an area where lesser black-backed gulls have been breeding for about seventy years. For landowners and their estate managers, the gulls are unwanted visitors and in recent years strenuous efforts have been made to deter them. Past measures have included attempts to destroy nests, the laying of bait poisoned with a narcotic (a previously legal remedy now proscribed by the government's rural affairs department Defra) and the use of falcons. So far, the gulls seem disinclined to take the hint and depart.

▶ Map continues eastwards on page 29

▶ Turn left to follow another fence as it crosses the moor almost due north to High Stephen's Head ❺. From here continue north-westwards, between a boundary fence and wall. This section of the walk is a delight, with the land falling down to both sides. To your right is the valley of the Roeburn, while to the left are the smaller cloughs which carry the waters of what will become Foxdale Beck. This stretch was inaccessible to the public before the introduction of access legislation.

Continue beside the fence, as the wall to your right disappears off towards Mallowdale. Follow the fence line all the way down, above the reedy waters of Ragill Beck. The route of the path can itself be wet in places.

As the fence briefly becomes a wall, cross Ragill Beck, and pick up the ill-defined track which runs down across the remaining moorland, to emerge through a farm gate above Deep Clough. Drop down into the clough (which is indeed very deep-cut at this point) and up the track the other side, to join the right of way coming in from the east ❻.

■ Quakerism, the popular name given to the Religious Society of Friends founded by George Fox (see pages 111–12), was for many years strong in parts of the Bowland area. Deep Clough Farm was the home of a very early Quaker family, the Thorntons, and Quaker meetings were held here at one time.

One issue which exercised early Quakers was how to arrange for the burial of their dead, since there was mutual antagonism between Quakers and the established Anglican church. Quakers denied that there was any particular holiness in officially consecrated ground, and in the early days of the movement they would generally arrange for burials to take place in gardens, orchards or fields owned by members. This was the arrangement at Deep Clough, where according to Quaker historian Donald Rooksby a small Quaker burial ground existed. At least two members of the Thornton family, and probably more, were buried

here in the early eighteenth century. Donald Rooksby reports that gravestones could still be found 'within living memory'.

▶ Having joined the footpath, follow it back down to river level, cross the small footbridge over a tributary of the main stream, and continue as the track once again climbs slightly up the hillside. (Following the riverside wall at this point involves getting wet and is not recommended.) In due course, the path drops yet again towards the river. This section of the route is pleasant woodland walking.

At Littledale Hall ❼, cross the river and turn left to make your way around the back of the extensive farm buildings. Here, look for a footpath arrow on a gate on your right. The footpath meanders through woodland before emerging near Field Head Farm.

■ The Littledale area is a particularly attractive part of countryside on the edge of the Bowland fells. Littledale Hall itself is a Victorian

building, built in the middle of the nineteenth century by John Dodson, from a Liverpool shipping family. Dodson also built the small

chapel at Crossgill, a short distance to the north.

▶ Continue along the right of way as it skirts Field Head Farm, turning left at Bellhill Farm. In due course, the path emerges beside Skelbow Barn **8**. Follow the path back up the hill to the starting point of the walk.

Blanch Fell

Bowland's bogs

Bowland has bogs: big gloopy peat bogs which can seize walkers' boots and wet squelchy mossy bogs into which the unwary can find themselves wandering.

But Bowland's bogs are important. Indeed, naturalists say that the blanket bogs in the Forest of Bowland, and also in the south Pennines, are of international conservation importance. Britain possesses about 10 per cent of the world's total area of blanket bog.

Why might you want to conserve bogs? For a host of reasons, according to English Nature. They provide a distinct habitat for bog-loving plants, most notably sphagnum moss but also the insect-eating sundew, bog rosemary and even the rare cloudberry plant. They keep the moors hydrated, preventing flash floods and helping to ensure that water taken off the moors for drinking is of a good quality. They provide places for insects such as cranefly to breed, and these in turn provide the food which baby grouse chicks need for the first few weeks of their lives. They also act as carbon sinks, their plants converting carbon dioxide into oxygen through photosynthesis. Britain may not have rain forests to help achieve this, but it has blanket bogs instead.

Unfortunately Bowland's bogs are under threat. A number of factors has meant that the number and quality of the high moorland blanket bogs have declined. Poorly managed heather burning has been one culprit. Another has been the efforts made to drain the moors, undertaken over the years by some estates in a (probably counterproductive) attempt to promote grouse numbers. A third, a perennial problem on the moors, has been overgrazing by sheep.

Together these measures have reduced the overall amount of water held on the moors, leading in some cases to the erosion of the thin top level of soil, which has simply been allowed to blow away. Where this has happened the familiar patches of dry crumbling peat, including sometimes deep haggs (banks), are left exposed ready to be churned up by walkers' boots.

English Nature also points the finger of blame at the activities of walkers. Because walkers have tended to follow fence boundaries, some strips of moorland in Bowland where they have done so have become badly eroded. One example is the ridge path from Totridge to Fiendsdale Head, which may in due course require remedial work (after some heart searching this route remains included in this book, but other areas of Bowland where there are important blanket bog habitats and where English Nature is keen to discourage walkers from visiting have been omitted).

Humans are also having an indirect effect on blanket bogs. Blanket bogs are naturally deficient in nutrients. However industrial pollution in the nineteenth and twentieth centuries, and now pollution from vehicles and agricultural fertilizers, have begun to change the nutrient balance, enriching the bogs and altering the nature of the vegetation which they can support. Sensitive species tend to lose out in these circumstances to more dominant plants.

So what does a healthy blanket bog look like? First, there are likely to be large quantities of moss, particularly sphagnum moss. Second, there will be a wide range of other bog plants flourishing. Third, bog pools will be abundant. And fourth, perhaps, there won't be too many walkers' bootprints: English Nature asks walkers to walk carefully on the moorland tops, and to steer clear of the main blanket bog areas.

WALK 2

HARRISEND FELL

DIFFICULTY  **DISTANCE** 3½ miles (6 km)

GRIZEDALE
BRIDGE

HARRISEND
FELL CAIRN

FELL END

GRIZEDALE
BRIDGE

MAP OS Explorer OL41, Forest of Bowland

STARTING POINT Car parking area close to Grizedale Bridge
(GR 536491)

PARKING There is room for a number of cars to park, on the
west side of the road near Grizedale Bridge.

PUBLIC TRANSPORT At the time of writing, Preston
Community Transport operates a community minibus service
(Mon–Sat) which serves Oakenclough from Garstang on a
pre-request only basis. Ring 01772 494989 to request the bus.
Oakenclough is about a mile (1.6 km) from the start of the walk.
See also page 66.

This short up-and-back
route includes some
rough walking and about
650 ft (190 m) of climb.

▶ From the road, follow one of
the paths up Harrisend Fell,
through the heather. Make for
the cairn at the fell top.

■ Harrisend Fell ❶ is an
attractive heather-clad grouse
moor to which the public
have had access only since
the implementation of the
Countryside and Rights of
Way Act 2000. The benefit
of climbing the fell is the view
which opens up, especially

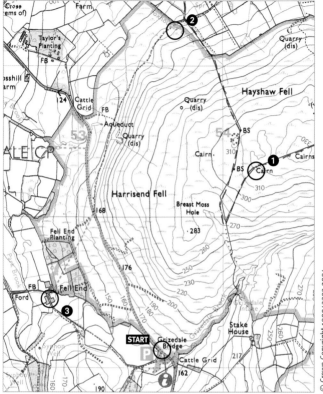

down over the Fylde area towards Blackpool. Obvious landmarks include Heysham nuclear power station, Lancaster University and the M6 motorway. Blackpool Tower may also be visible.

▶ At this point, to make a longer walk, it's possible to continue across Hayshaw Fell to Grizedale Head, returning for example by the Catshaw Fell shooting track. The suggested route for this walk, however, involves a direct descent down the northern side of Harrisend Fell, close to the boundary fence between Harrisend and Hayshaw Fells. This ground is somewhat rough and wet in places.

As pastures begin on your right, look for the waymarked footpath which crosses the moor ❷. Turn left on to the path, and follow it as it contours around the side of the fell. Continue across the road and head for Fell End Farm ❸.

■ Short-eared owls are among the birds which can be sighted in the Harrisend Fell area.

▶ Another optional extension to this walk is available at Fell End Farm, by taking the footpath through the farm which leads towards the outlying fell Nicky Nook and the woods near Grizedale reservoir.

Otherwise, turn left in the farmyard, to find the bridleway that heads back towards Grizedale Bridge.

A misty day near the Cross of Greet

Sorry, I haven't a clough

One thing that speakers of southern English will discover if they go walking in the hills in the north country is that steep-sided valleys and ravines have a word of their own: clough. It's the word which gives us the familiar Clough surname and of course it's pronounced 'cluff'.

Or at least it is in most parts of northern England. But the Forest of Bowland is a place apart. Bowland certainly has its cloughs, many of them – Greave Clough, Hunter's Clough, Blind Clough, Well Brook Clough, Black Clough and a host of others, all denoting the little valleys taking water off the high moor ground. But the Bowland difference is that a clough is pronounced 'cloo'.

Somewhere in this part of Lancashire, in other words, is an invisible line which travellers unknowingly cross, the line which marks 'cluff' land from 'cloo' land. Linguists have a name for such boundaries ('isogloss'), and even if the 'cluff'/'cloo' isogloss is rather less dramatic than the famous north/south divides between the long and the short 'a' (castle) and the clipped and the rounded 'u' (up), it's still the sort of dialectal quirk which makes the English language such a fertile area to explore.

Quite where 'cloo' stops and 'cluff' starts is hard to say. One of the main twentieth-century studies into regional pronunciations and word usages was the Survey of English Dialects. This work, based at the University of Leeds, took place between 1948 and 1961 and involved fieldworkers going out to talk to people in over 300 mainly rural parts of England and recording what they said. The Survey can help identify all sorts of interesting isoglosses (which regions say 'room' with a short vowel and which with a long vowel, for example, or the different regional pronunciations of the word Tuesday). One thing the

Survey of English Dialects didn't think to ask informants, however, was what word they would use to describe a steep-sided valley or ravine and how they would pronounce it.

'Cloo' is certainly not to be found very widely in Lancashire. Derek Stanton, a folk singer and broadcaster who is an active member of the Lancashire Dialect Society, comes from Preston and says firmly that he would say 'cluff'. His colleague in the Lancashire Dialect Society Dr Peter Wright has written and lectured on Lancashire speech, and he too says he is not familiar with the 'cloo' pronunciation.

The –ough ending in English is, of course, the famous anomaly in pronunciation – just try rhyming bough, cough, rough, through and thorough. Part of the problem is that English used to have a convenient letter, the yogh (it looked a little like ʒ), which could represent a slightly more guttural version of the Scottish 'ch' sound. When the yogh disappeared from use, early printers made do as best they could, often with some variation on a –gh spelling. If we still had a yogh today, we would probably spell clough as cloʒ.

But that still doesn't explain the variations in pronunciation. Over the centuries, according to the *Oxford English Dictionary*, clough has been spelled in many different ways: clough, cloff, cloughe, clowgh, clow and cloh, to give just a few examples. These spellings suggest that the word sometimes was given a final 'ff' sound and sometimes wasn't.

Ultimately, we probably just have to go along with the words of Geoffrey Chaucer, writing in the late fourteenth century, when as he put it 'ther is so gret diversite In Englissh and in writing of oure tonge'.

There is rather more consensus about another aspect of pronunciation, and that is the proper local way to say 'Bowland'. Forget any thoughts about archers and bows and arrows. The area is traditionally the Forest of *Bolland*, the first syllable probably deriving from the Norse word for cattle.

WALK 3

HAWTHORNTHWAITE

DIFFICULTY 👢 👢 👢 **DISTANCE 8 miles (13 km)**

CAM CLOUGH (ABBEYSTEAD) — CATSHAW GREAVE — GREAVE CLOUGH HEAD — HAWTHORN-THWAITE FELL TOP — BLACK CLOUGH — MARSHAW — CAM CLOUGH

MAP OS Explorer OL41, Forest of Bowland

STARTING POINT On the back road between Marshaw and Wyresdale/Garstang, south of Abbeystead village

PARKING One of the best places to park is beside Cam Clough, at GR 563528.

PUBLIC TRANSPORT In recent years, a grant-funded rural bus service B15 has run through the Trough of Bowland twice daily on Sundays and Bank Holidays. However, the future of this service is not secure. In addition, at the time of writing, Preston Community Transport operates a community minibus service (Mon–Sat) which serves Abbeystead from Garstang on an occasional basis on a pre-request only basis. Ring 01772 494989 to request the bus. Abbeystead is about a mile (1.6 km) from the start of the walk. See also page 66.

This walk visits a little-explored area of the southern Bowland fells. Some wet ground and rough moorland walking.

▶ Walk south-westwards along the quiet back road, passing the drive to Fellside Farm. Take the shooting track up the side of Catshaw Greave.

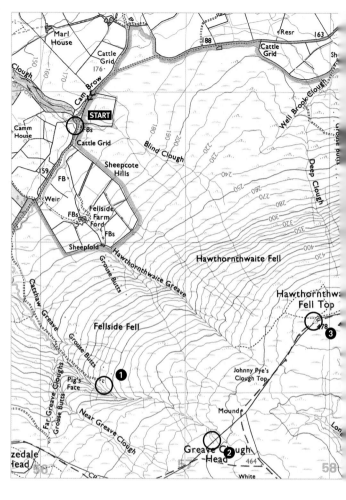

When the track stops **1**, just beyond interestingly named Pig's Face, continue up the left side of the clough. It may be possible to find a trod (faint path) here to assist you. At the top, you will emerge on to the soggy ground of Greave Clough Head **2**.

Follow the boundary fence round to the left. The ground here

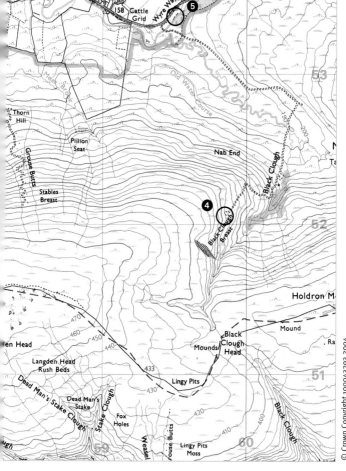

© Crown Copyright 100043293 2004

is, in places, quite wet and boggy. After about ½ mile (just over 1 km), you will reach Hawthornthwaite Fell Top ❸.

■ In any competition between the trig points of Bowland for good views or interesting surroundings, poor old Hawthornthwaite

Fell Top would end up with *nul points*. The problem here, as will readily become apparent, is the erosion which has taken place on the summit plateau. The trig point itself is now an absurd sight, marooned many feet above ground level on a precarious pillar of stone.

Peat represents the remains of moorland vegetation which has been deposited on these hills since the last Ice Age some 14,000 years ago, and which in places can be up to 20 ft (6 m) in depth. The bare peat becomes exposed as a result of erosion of surface vegetation (see pages 32–3).

▶ From Hawthornthwaite Fell Top, the aim is to head roughly due east for a little over a mile (about 2 km), to pick up the estate shooting track close to Black Clough Breast ❹. This has previously been a challenging task, with rough walking, but Lancashire County Council has now helped by waymarking a recommended route.

Once reached, the estate track provides easy walking down the side of Black Clough, to emerge on to the main Trough of Bowland road at Marshaw ❺.

■ The unprepossessing little patch of land at Marshaw was the location for a ceremony arranged by the Countryside Agency on Sunday 19 September 2004 to mark the introduction of the access provisions of the Countryside and Rights of Way Act 2000. The event took place,

significantly, on the Duke of Westminster's Abbeystead estate; this estate had previously been particularly targeted by ramblers campaigning for access to open country.

▶ From Marshaw, a concessionary footpath in the fields beside the river provides a temporary respite from road walking. From the T-junction at Marshaw, however, there is little option but to walk on tarmac back to the starting point of the walk.

■ Over to the right is Abbeystead Hall, the stately home which is the Duke of Westminster's base when he is visiting his estate. The house, set in fine grounds, was built in the late nineteenth century for the Earl of Sefton, then owner of the Abbeystead estate.

The Hodder valley and the Bowland fells

Getting ready for access

Carefully, delicately, the helicopter lowered its load on to the designated point high up on the open Bowland fells, flew off and returned a little later with a second load, ready for delivery to another nearby area of moorland. It was just before Easter in 2004, and this helicopter activity over Bowland was visible evidence that the right to roam the moors would soon become a reality.

The helicopter had been called in by Lancashire County Council's Countryside Service, as the easiest way to convey sets of gates and stiles on to the high moors. In some places field gates were deposited on the heather and peat, in other places timber needed to make kissing gates or ladder stiles, but in each case the aim was the same: to create openings in what had previously been unbroken lines of boundary walls and fences, in order to enable walkers to make their way unimpeded across the hills.

The arrival of the helicopter with its loads was the culmination of a careful process of preparation for open access which began after the passing of the Countryside and Rights of Way Act in 2000 and which was led in the Forest of Bowland by Lancashire's Countryside Service. In order to know where to put the gates and stiles, it had to try to guess where the public would choose to wander. Some routes – such as those along ridges or up to trig points and summits – might be fairly easy to predict, but elsewhere the task was more challenging. And there were other things which needed to be taken into account: where would walkers coming by car find parking places, for example? Where should information boards or access signs be best positioned?

Part of the Forest of Bowland area was selected, with the support of the national Countryside Agency, for an early pilot project. To discuss what needed to be done, the county brought together a small group of interested people: Bowland landowners, staff from English Nature (with their particular concerns about nature conservation) and a representative of walking groups. The council's plans gradually took shape, and by early 2004 the countryside service had produced a detailed map of Bowland, complete with what it called likely 'desire lines' for routes across the fells. The map, and the routes of these 'desire lines', were only for internal council use but enabled the exact locations for each gate and stile to be decided.

Not everything was plain sailing, however. One continuing issue in Bowland is that access land does not always abut public roads or existing rights of way. Certain private roads, including shooting tracks, were identified early on as convenient access routes for the public into the open countryside – but while some landowners were happy for their roads to be used in this way, in other cases there was reluctance. Every successful negotiation had to be followed up by a formal agreement.

What has become available over the relatively short time since access rights have been in force may, therefore, be added to as time goes by. In fact, it will probably be several years before the practical process of implementing access in Bowland has been fully worked through.

Lancashire County Council has had the advantage of a long history of work to encourage access. Using powers available to it under post-war legislation it negotiated in the 1970s a series of access agreements to relatively small parts of the Bowland moors: to Clougha in the north and to Fair Snape, Saddle Fell and Wolf Fell in the south. (Later, in the 1990s, a further agreement opened up White Moor to public access.) Similar agreements were made in other parts of the county, including the West Pennine Moors and the Boulsworth moors near Burnley. These formal agreements – unlike those made as a result of the new access legislation approved in 2000 – involved paying public money to landowners or tenants in compensation.

Even under the new legislation, however, access to the moors is not precisely free. Lancashire's Countryside Service points out that each of its new gates and stiles involved expenditure: about £400 to install a kissing gate in a drystone wall, for instance, and up to £300 for a field gate in a fence. These payments, the expenditure for access signs and the larger 'interpretation boards' now in place in major car parking areas and all the other costs associated with implementing the access legislation were met partly from a grant from the Countryside Agency and partly by the county council itself.

After all this work and expenditure, what is now in place is the infrastructure to enable walkers to enjoy the high Bowland fells for years to come: it seems a small cost to set against the enormous pleasure which many people will be able to take from discovering this corner of Lancashire for themselves.

WALK 4

BLEASDALE AND FAIR SNAPE

DIFFICULTY 👢 👢 👢 **DISTANCE 11 miles (17.5 km)**

DELPH QUARRY	STANG YULE	BLEASDALE MOORS	FIENDSDALE HEAD	FAIR SNAPE FELL	PARLICK	BLEASDALE VILLAGE	DELPH QUARRY

MAP OS Explorer OL41, Forest of Bowland

STARTING POINT Delph Quarry, Delph Lane, Bleasdale (GR 546455)

PARKING In the Delph car park

PUBLIC TRANSPORT At the time of writing, Preston Community Transport operates a community minibus service (Mon–Sat) which serves Calder Vale (about 1 mile/1.6 km away by field footpaths). Ring 01772 494989 for information. See also page 66.

A delightful horseshoe of ridge walking, followed by a few miles of pleasant footpaths leading across farmland. Fair Snape Fell and Parlick has become one of the most popular walking areas in Bowland. This walk completes a classic circular walk by adding in Hazelhurst Fell and Winny Bank, not publicly accessible before 2004. A little rough open moorland walking.

▶ From the car park, walk north along Delph Lane to the Stang Yule corner and turn right ❶. Walk towards the house, turning up the track which leads to the

▶ page 50

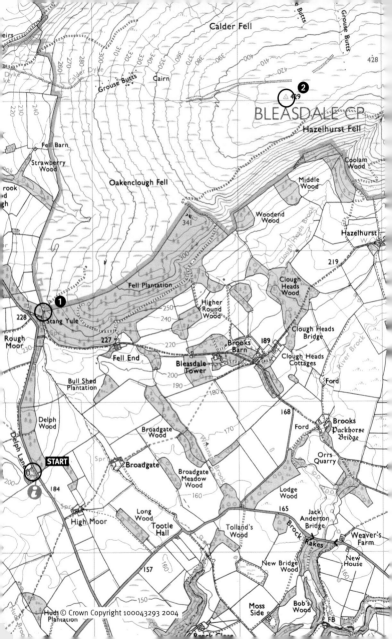

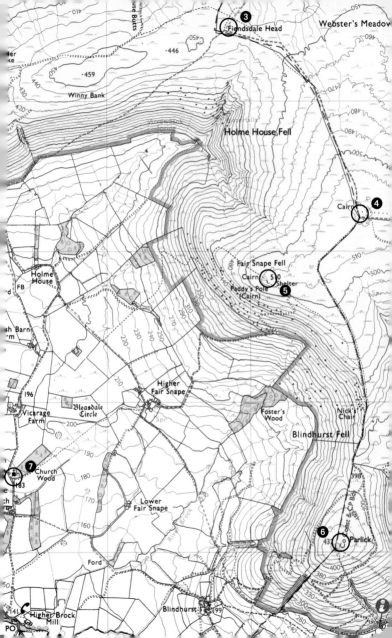

open moors. Follow the rough track as it winds its way up the hillside, running close to the boundary wall of Fell Plantation.

■ This fine stretch of heather grouse moor has been managed by the Bleasdale estate, and the track (unlike shooting tracks on some other Bowland estates) is pleasant, unobtrusive and easy walking.

▶ Continue up the track past the end of the plantation, on to the slopes of Hazelhurst Fell. Fine views open up, both across to Fair Snape Fell and Parlick and down into the Bleasdale valley to the right.

After another ¾ mile (1.2 km) or so, there is the option of taking a track which heads up the hill to the left, leading almost to the trig point at the top of the hill ❷. If you choose to visit the trig point, the best alternative is probably to retrace your steps back down to the original track.

The track loses some height as it swings down to cross little Clough Heads Brook, and then

climbs again, meeting another track coming in from the direction of Hazelhurst. Once more, follow the track up,

heading round the side of the high ground of Winny Bank.

Eventually, after perhaps 3 miles (4.8 km) of easy walking from Stang Yule, it is time to leave the track. The next ⅓ mile (0.5 km) heads across open moorland. This used to be a

Walker on Parlick Hill

difficult task; however, waymarks have now been put in place, to make the route easier to follow.

You reach the boundary fence ahead near the ladder stile at Fiendsdale Head ❸.

■ Fiendsdale Head is an important crossroads for walkers. A footpath from Hazelhurst comes in from the right, and continues over the stile down the side of Fiendsdale Water to Langden Castle (visited in Walk 5).

Fiendsdale also marks the limit of the original Fair Snape access land, which was opened to the public under an agreement negotiated between the landowner and Lancashire County Council.

▶ Ignore the path heading across the moor to Fiendsdale Water, and follow the fence boundary as it runs round the top of Home House Fell. There are paths on both sides of the fence, and the choice is yours. Both paths are in places wet and involve negotiating peat haggs; of the two, the path beyond the fence is perhaps better. The fence leads

in due course to a set of cairns, marking the highest point of Fair Snape Fell, 1707 ft (320 m) ❹.

Continue briefly alongside the fence which runs off in a south-westerly direction, but leave it shortly to make for the large cairn known as Paddy's Pole ❺.

■ Paddy's Pole gives its name to an annual fell race, which starts at the public car park at Fell Foot near Chipping, and involves a climb of 1100 ft (330 m) to Parlick and Fair Snape followed by a mad downhill dash back to the starting point – a round trip of about $4\frac{1}{2}$ miles (7.2 km). The course record is currently set at about thirty-one minutes.

Between Paddy's Pole and the OS trig point is a curious stone-built wind shelter, made up of four neatly constructed 'cubicles' – obviously built for walkers who prefer not to talk to their neighbours while eating their sandwiches.

▶ From Fair Snape, a well-walked path heads off across the grass towards Parlick, the final summit ❻.

■ The conical shape of Parlick makes it a landmark when viewed from outside Bowland, though the summit itself, bisected by a fence, is rather disappointing.

▶ Drop down the hillside from Parlick, making for the large farm of Blindhurst. From the edge of the access land, a concessionary path leads down directly into the farm. Pass through the farmyard, and take the field footpath which runs north-eastwards towards Bleasdale school. At the school, turn right to follow the track to Bleasdale church ❼.

■ According to local historian Jean Fone, the people of Bleasdale were described in 1340 by the Abbot of Whalley as 'few, intractable and wild'. Efforts to educate Bleasdale's children began early, with a bequest given by a local landowner in 1702 of £10 a year for a schoolmaster for the village – although it seems that he did not always manage the job particularly well. Jean Fone reports how,

in Victorian times, one curate called Mr Birkett 'gave a very good sermon but seemed unable to control the pupils'.

The current Bleasdale church dates from 1835, although there was a church hereabouts from the late sixteenth century. It is the only church dedicated to St Eadmer, a tenth-century monk whose sole claim to fame is that he was indirectly responsible for the building of Durham cathedral. After the death of the great St Cuthbert of Lindisfarne Northumbrian monks were unsure where he should be buried until Eadmer received a vision, advising him that Cuthbert's body should be taken to Durham.

Bleasdale's main point of interest, however, is the Bleasdale circle. This is an archaeological site dating back to the Bronze Age, which was discovered and excavated by two archaeologists in 1898–1900 and was re-excavated in the 1930s. 'Bleasdale circle' is perhaps a misleading name, for this could suggest a henge-type structure such as Stonehenge. What was found was rather more complicated.

The archaeologists discovered a central burial mound, within which were two cremation urns with the remains of bones. These are similar to other Bronze Age cremation urns, and are now kept at the Harris museum in Preston.

The mound was surrounded by a ditch about 3 ft (0.9 m) deep and approaching 4 ft (1.2 m) wide. Surrounding this, in turn, was a circle of eleven large oak posts, making up a sort of palisade, with some smaller posts set between them.

What archaeologists don't know is the relationship of the mound to the wooden circle. One theory is that the wooden posts were a much earlier construction, dating from neolithic times (c. 4000–c. 2000 BC), which had disappeared by the time the burial mound was built.

A display board near the parish hall gives further information and arrangements for visiting the circle.

▶ From the church, take the footpath past Admarsh barn towards Brooks. Here note the old packhorse bridge over the Brock river, to your right. Continue to Brooks Barn, and there turn half-left, taking the footpath which runs across fields past the frontage of Bleasdale Tower, towards Broadgate and High Moor farms. Beyond High Moor, you reach the road, a short distance from Delph Quarry.

■ The walk begins and ends at a tautology: a delph is a quarry.

Managing the moors

To some, the Bowland moors may seem like pristine wilderness, land which has been created by nature and left untamed by human activity.

But actually, they aren't like that at all. The moors may not be farmed in conventional terms, but they are nevertheless places of economic activity where a form of agriculture – or at least land management – is practised week in week out, and where a sizeable number of people earn their living. Understanding this shouldn't detract from the experience of walking the fells. In fact, our pleasure should be enhanced if we can put the landscape in its proper context.

The main purpose of managing the moors is for the grouse. There are two major landowners in Bowland and a number of somewhat smaller estates, and for all of them grouse shooting is important. The Abbeystead estate owns a great swathe of moorland on the western side of the main Bowland watershed, including the Clougha, Tarnbrook, Hawthornthwaite and Mallowdale fells. On the other side of the watershed is another large estate held by United Utilities (formerly North West Water), which was acquired as a water catchment area but where shooting rights are also important.

The land which now forms the Abbeystead estate was originally put together by the Sixth Earl of Sefton in the late nineteenth century, when Abbeystead House was also constructed. This was the time when driven grouse shooting was developing as an upper-class pursuit, in part as a result of changes in gun technology. In 1980, executors of the Sefton family estate put Abbeystead up for sale, and all 18,000 acres passed to the Duke of Westminster (or technically, as pointed out in the introduction, to a family trust which is linked to the Duke of Westminster).

The duke and his family normally spend a summer holiday at Abbeystead House, coinciding with the start of the grouse shooting season on 12 August. But the estate itself is managed from a small office near by, where Rod Banks, the estate manager, has his place of work. Rod Banks originally trained as an accountant but has spent most of his working life at Abbeystead, including more than twenty-five years as estate manager. Looking after the estate (which has grown through further acquisitions to 23,000 acres) involves overseeing the work of thirty staff, including ten gamekeepers, four foresters, maintenance workers and a number of gardeners and household staff for Abbeystead House.

Abbeystead is both an agricultural and a shooting estate. On the agricultural side, the estate is landlord to a number of local tenant farmers and the aim is to run a profitable commercial business. But it is the shooting side of the estate which is the real heart of the operation, and normal business rules about profitability apply much less strongly to this. What is more important is to ensure that there is good shooting to be had.

In his office, Rod Banks keeps custody of what he calls the bible – the Game Book, which records all the grouse taken on all the shoots going back to the earliest days of the estate. Here, for example, can be found the record of the astonishing day's shooting in 1915 when the sky was black with birds and a shooting party (eight 'guns', as always) brought down 2929 birds, an Abbeystead (and world) record. Here, too, are more recent records, including three lean years when grouse numbers were too low to risk any shooting at all.

Grouse are wild birds, which breed naturally (unlike other game birds, such as pheasants, for which breeding pens can be used), and their numbers fluctuate naturally, on roughly a seven-year cycle. But this statement needs qualifying. One aim of a well-run shooting estate is to manage the moors in such a way that the grouse have the best possible chance of multiplying. This means, for instance, setting snares and traps to remove potential predators such as stoats, weasels, rats and crows. (This, it should be said, is perfectly legal.) It means managing the heather. Grouse like young heather shoots best, so roughly every five years the old, bushy heather is burnt back in controlled burning operations.

It also means trying to keep the grouse healthy. Grouse have a problem with their insides, or more precisely with intestinal worms which take up residence in them. The little trays of grouse grit which can be found all over grouse moors are one answer: the grit aids grouse digestion, and it is often medicated specifically to tackle the worms.

Then there are ticks, lurking in bracken ready to be picked up by passing sheep. Sheep ticks cause a nasty viral disease called louping ill. Louping ill is a hazard for humans, since it can cause encephalitis (swelling of the brain), but it is particularly nasty if you happen to be a grouse chick. One test found that four in five grouse chicks with the virus died.

The Abbeystead estate tries various ways of keeping ticks at bay. Areas of bracken where ticks like to linger are regularly destroyed using aerial spraying. The local sheep population is also regularly dipped: the estate pays for two extra sheep dips each year, to try to eradicate the ticks.

There are other natural hazards. In recent years, the growing numbers of the little green-brown heather beetle (*Lochmaea suturalis*) have been causing concern, particularly in Scotland and Wales. The beetle eats its way through heather, and a bad infestation can turn a healthy purple heather moorland brown. Abbeystead estate says that, touch wood, it currently has *Lochmaea suturalis* under control.

But 'grouse production', as Rod Banks calls it, ultimately depends on the birds themselves. Typically, the nests are made and eggs laid in April, with fledgling chicks hatching in mid-May.

For the first few days of their lives, the chicks rely on insects, which can be in short supply if the weather is particularly dry. (Very wet weather during the breeding season is also bad news.)

Come mid-July each year it is time to check the year's crop of birds. The Abbeystead estate arranges for pointers to be sent into the heather to flush out the birds, so that a rough count can be undertaken. From this, the estate manager and gamekeeper estimate how many days' shooting are likely to be possible. Although officially the grouse season runs until 10 December, in practice shooting will carry on beyond September only in good years. A poor season means disappointment all round, as well as a lower income for the estate (a party of eight 'guns' arranging a day's shooting in Bowland might pay as much as £20,000 between them for the privilege; and, incidentally, the shot grouse remain the property of the estate).

But the climax of all the hard work, and expenditure, is the 'Glorious Twelfth', when the season starts and when, at Abbeystead, the Duke of Westminster and his guests will be conveyed to each of the main grouse driving areas on the estate to see what they can bag. This is, ultimately, why the moors are managed, this is why the keepers are out in all weathers laying and checking traps, burning the heather, putting down the grouse grit. Shooting may be an activity which many find incomprehensible, but it's hard to understand life on the Bowland fells without understanding the key role which it plays.

WALK 5

BLEADALE WATER

DIFFICULTY 🥾 🥾 🥾 🥾 **DISTANCE 8½ miles (13.7 km)**

TROUGH OF BOWLAND (LANGDEN BROOK) — HAREDEN — TOTRIDGE — BLEADALE WATER — LANGDEN CASTLE — TROUGH OF BOWLAND

MAP OS Explorer OL41, Forest of Bowland

STARTING POINT Car parking area in the woods at Langden Brook on the Trough of Bowland road (GR 632512)

PARKING This is a popular place for picnickers, with space for a significant number of cars.

PUBLIC TRANSPORT In recent years, the grant-funded rural bus service B15 has run through the Trough of Bowland twice daily on Sundays and Bank Holidays. However, the future of this service is not secure. See also page 66.

A fine walk into the wild heart of Bowland, with the highlight being the gradual descent of beautiful Bleadale. However, please bear in mind the following points: first, the ridge footpath beyond Totridge is badly eroded, and walkers are asked to avoid using it when the ground is likely to be particularly wet. Second, two streams have to be forded near Langden Castle – and crossing these is not recommended when the rivers are in spate or after heavy rain.

▶ Take the concessionary footpath beside Langden Brook south-east towards Hareden.

■ The building which you can see across the river is a base for the Bowland Pendle Mountain Rescue Team. Like other mountain rescue teams, Bowland Pendle operates on an entirely voluntary basis, and has about forty members currently actively available for emergency call-outs.

Anyone venturing on to the Bowland fells has cause to be grateful that the team are available for emergencies. Each year sees a number of walkers, including in some instances well-equipped and experienced hill walkers, get into difficulties, perhaps because of an accident or a rapid deterioration in weather conditions. A typical example for the team was the rescue which took place early in 2004 of a man in his twenties, who had planned to walk on the fells for about three hours and who was finally rescued at 10pm in

▶ page 64

© Crown Copyright 100043293 2004

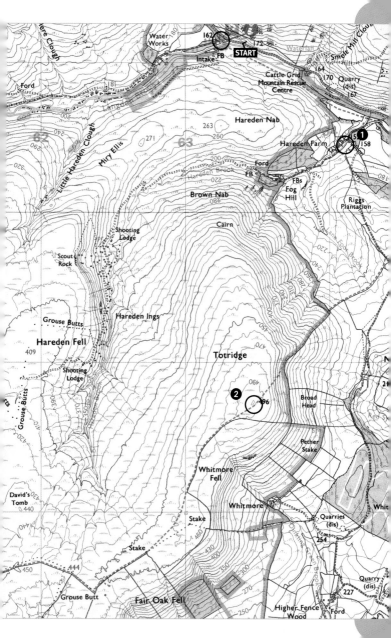

Langden Brook

sub-zero temperatures, having spent ten hours disorientated and lost. He used a mobile phone to call for help, saying he was stranded on Wolf Fell. In fact, he was found 3 miles (4.8 km) away, on Luddock's Fell. His experience is a reminder for all walkers of the potential dangers of the open fells.

Bowland Pendle MRT also assist the police and other emergency services throughout the Lancashire area. They were called out, for example, to help during the Morecambe Bay cockle-picking tragedy that took place in February 2004.

The name of the building used by Bowland Pendle MRT, Smelt Mill, recalls the fact that smelting of lead mined near Brennand Farm was an important activity for several centuries. The lead industry continued until late in the nineteenth century.

▶ At Hareden ❶, make for the summit of Totridge, either taking the bridleway south from Hareden Farm or by following the water company road slightly further and making your way over open ground. This is a stiff climb: in total, the height difference from the walk's start is almost 1100 ft (about 330 m). The concessionary footpath up the slope of Totridge offers the easiest way up ❷.

■ Totridge provides views east towards Easington Fell and Pendle Hill, and south to Longridge.

This is one of the best places to look down on the peaceful valley of the Hodder (walk a little south from the trig point for the best views).

The Hodder is associated with the nineteenth-century poet Gerard Manley Hopkins, who lived for a time at Stoneyhurst College just to the south of the Forest of Bowland.

Hopkins celebrates the natural beauty of the area in a number of his poems and writings. It is easy to imagine that it is the Hodder which Hopkins is describing, with his customary linguistic exuberance, in his poem 'Epithalamion':

> . . . *where a candycoloured,*
> *where a gluegold-brown*
> *Marbled river, boisterously*
> *beautiful, between*
> *Roots and rocks is danced*
> *and dandled, all in froth*
> *and water-blowballs,*
> *down.*

▶ Continue from Totridge south-westwards, taking the concessionary path which follows the boundary fence along the fell top. This path, particularly at the edge of Saddle Fell, has become eroded and there are deep peat haggs and bogs to be negotiated.

Struggle on along the fence above Saddle Fell, looking out for a stone inscribed WD31. This was one of a series of marker stones erected by the War Department who used the moors for training during the Second World War. Just past here, a small stream disappears down the hillside to the right. A faint path ❸ runs alongside it: take this. If you are right, you will find that the path quickly becomes much more defined. (If you miss the turn,

you will very shortly arrive at a ladder stile, offering access over the fence on to Saddle Fell. Turn back!)

Follow the path down the side of Bleadale Water. Initially the path jumps from one side of the stream to the other, before settling down to follow the right-hand bank. The valley is one of the wildest and most beautiful areas of Bowland.

The path descends beside Bleadale Water, with the valley gradually opening up. Eventually the stone hut known as Langden Castle comes into sight. Choose a place to ford both Bleadale Water and Langden Brook.

■ Langden Castle ❹ suggests something rather more exciting than the building itself can deliver. It was probably built a century or so ago for shooting parties. Another 'castle' near by, Holdron Castle, is equally unfortified, being an outcrop of rocks.

▶ From Langden Castle follow the well-made track back to the starting point of the walk.

Public transport in the Forest of Bowland

As in other rural areas, bus services in the more isolated areas of the Forest of Bowland cannot easily be run on a commercial basis and financial support, from central or local government, is required. Unfortunately, this means that bus services can be under threat as a result of funding cut-backs or changes in funding policy.

At the time of writing, buses to Slaidburn/Newton from Clitheroe and Settle together with the Trough of Bowland Sunday service are provided by Bowland Transit, a community-based project which has received Rural Bus Challenge funding but whose long-term future is unclear. Another current initiative in the Clitheroe and eastern Bowland area comes from Ribble Valley Community Transport which offers a dial-a-bus taxi-type service (01200 444484). In western Bowland, Preston Community Transport currently operates 'Super8' community bus services from Garstang.

There can be no guarantee that these services will remain unchanged. For up-to-date information, it is worth checking at local information centres or on the Internet.

The centre of
the kingdom

As probably even the locals would admit, the Forest of Bowland doesn't feel as though it is at the centre of anything. It's something of a surprise, therefore, to be told when you arrive at Dunsop Bridge that you are now in the village at 'the centre of Britain'.

This is the message which will greet you, for example, in the village's tea room and shop. It's also proudly emblazoned on BT's public phone box on the village green, which is adorned with arrows from Dunsop Bridge to various other places in the country. BT likes to say that, in honour of Dunsop Bridge's claim to fame, it awarded the village its 100,000th phone box, though it's not quite clear who was counting (currently BT has about 70,000 call boxes in Britain).

Sadly, whichever way you work it out, Dunsop Bridge's phone box isn't really central to anything. But it is indeed true, or sort of, that just a few miles north of Dunsop Bridge on the open moors is a patch of peaty bog which can lay claim to being at the centre of the kingdom. Which particular patch of peat is a more difficult question to answer.

The idea is relatively simple to understand: if you were to cut out the shape of Great Britain in cardboard and balance it on a pin, this is the point where the pin would have to be put. The calculation using this 'gravitational method' was first done by Ordnance Survey more than ten years ago – and since then, OS has probably wished many times that it hadn't bothered. Every few years the story is picked up again by the media, public interest – and controversy – is re-ignited, and OS has to take the time and effort to explain exactly how it did its sums. And yet, one OS spokesperson wearily said, 'This sort of information is completely irrelevant to us as cartographers.'

One difficulty for OS is that you can do all sorts of calculations and come up with different answers. If you just work out the gravitational balancing point of the British mainland (England, Scotland and Wales without any of the islands), the centre ends up, according to the OS, at grid reference 72321 36671 – or unpleasantly close to the sewage works on the outskirts of Whalley, Lancs. Add in the seven large inshore islands (Anglesey, Arran, Mull, Skye, Jura, Islay and the Isle of Wight), and the centre moves a little further west and north, to GR 68123 41406, an area of woodland near Longridge. But if you take into account all the 401 islands of any note surrounding the shore of Great Britain – and arguably this is the big one, the one which really matters – you arrive at a point a few yards or metres to the west of the Whitendale Hanging Stones, a little over four miles (six and a half kilometres) north of Dunsop Bridge. The full grid reference, according to the OS website, is SD 64188.30 56541.43.

Unfortunately, the story now gets even more complicated. Some time in the past ten years, a slightly different grid reference to this one started to be publicized. This one was SD 63770 56550, which would shift the centre of Britain about a quarter of a mile or four hundred metres further to the west, very close to the wet ground marked on maps as Brown Syke Moss. This is the grid reference which has been given in a number of guidebooks.

OS is at a loss to explain quite how this discrepancy developed, but the sad fact is that many people who in recent years waded through the peat to stand at what they thought was the central point of Britain may have got it wrong.

One of the walks in this book, Walk 6, will take you up the moorland fence boundary very close to the correct spot – though there is nothing there at present to tell you that you have arrived. And if you were thinking of relying on a GPS device to locate the exact ten-centimetre square identified by the grid reference, OS has an additional word of caution for you. Grid references, it points out, are devised from the national grid; GPS devices use a different coordinate system. Bringing the two systems together can cause minor discrepancies. Normally these aren't enough to worry about; nevertheless, they could mean that a GPS reading will identify an area which is some yards or metres away from the actual grid reference site. Finding the real centre of Britain is clearly a troublesome business.

None of this is at all relevant, of course, if you reject the pin-and-cardboard type of approach to calculating the centre of the land. The BBC has publicized a rival claim which has been advanced by the town of Haltwhistle in Northumberland, while the place furthest from the sea – yet another possible way of defining Britain's centre – turns out to be near the village of Coton in the Elms, Derbyshire.

Northern Ireland, by the way, isn't taken into account in any of these calculations.

Somewhere near the centre of Britain. The pole marks nothing more than a grouse-grit tray.

WALK 6

WOLFHOLE CRAG

DIFFICULTY 🥾 🥾 🥾 🥾 **DISTANCE 11 miles (17.5 km)**

TROUGH OF BOWLAND — BRENNAND FARM — WHITENDALE HANGING STONES — WOLFHOLE CRAG — BRENNAND GREAT HILL — MILLER'S HOUSE — WHINS BROW — TROUGH OF BOWLAND

MAP OS Explorer OL41, Forest of Bowland

STARTING POINT At the summit of the Trough of Bowland road (beside Grey Stone of Trough boundary stone), GR 623530

PARKING Parking is available for about four cars just to the west of the summit.

PUBLIC TRANSPORT In recent years, the grant-funded rural bus service B15 has run through the Trough of Bowland twice daily on Sundays and Bank Holidays. However, the future of this service is not secure. See also page 66.

A tough moorland walk, with much rough walking through wet ground, but with the compensation of visiting the 'centre of Britain'.

■ This walk begins and ends beside the Grey Stone of Trough, the boundary stone which has been in this spot since it was put up in 1897. The Grey Stone is a reminder that, though today we seem to be deep in the heart of Lancashire, until local government reform in 1974 this was the dividing line between Lancashire and Yorkshire. The West Riding of Yorkshire swept up and around the Burnley and Pendle area to take much of the eastern side of Bowland, including the settlements of Slaidburn, Dunsop Bridge, Whitewell, Newton and Waddington.

Evidence of Yorkshire's role in Bowland can be found in various places: one of the most obvious is on the bridge over the Ribble between Clitheroe and Waddington, which still informs travellers coming from the east that – counterintuitively – they are crossing from Lancashire to Yorkshire. Waddington commemorates its Yorkshire past on its village sign, where the red rose of Lancashire is combined with Yorkshire's white rose.

▶ From the starting point, follow the road for about ⅔ mile (1 km) towards Dunsop Bridge, and then take the bridleway at Trough Barn ❶. This well-walked path climbs steadily, past the ruins of Trough House on to the side of Whin Fell. By the time you reach the brow, you will have climbed about 735 ft (220 m).

■ Pause at the hill brow ❷, where – provided the weather is fair – you will be able to see before you much of the rest of the route of this walk. The summit of Wolfhole Crag is visible high up to the north, while to its left is the boundary fence past Brennand Great Hill which marks the return route.

Brennand Farm was once a medieval vaccary, or in other words a settlement where cattle were reared. Later the area became a centre for mining, with lead ore being removed from the hills from the seventeenth century until the late nineteenth century. Silver is also reported to have been extracted. Although most of the signs of this industrial past have disappeared, there are still remains to be found by those prepared to search.

▶ Sadly, almost all the height gained in the climb from the Trough of Bowland road now has to be lost in the descent to Brennand Farm ❸. The right of way runs through the farmyard, and then turns left to cross Brennand River by a bridge.

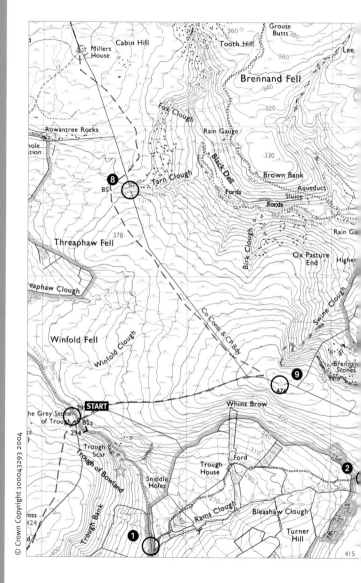

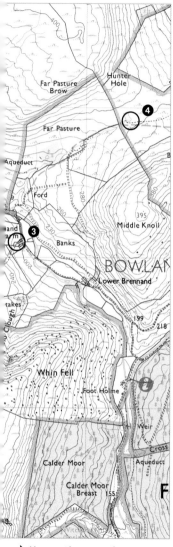

Continue on the right of way up the hill beyond Brennand, following the waymark signs until you approach the small tarn shown on the map. This was in fact a reservoir constructed as part of the mining operations.

■ At this point **4** you enter access land, and can turn left straight up the hillside to Hunter Hole, keeping the boundary wall initially to your left (a gate in the wall ahead allows access to the fells beyond). Carry on beside the moorland fence, until it bends slightly to the right just before Whitendale Hanging Stones **5**. At an appropriate moment cross to the other side of the fence.

The story of how grid reference SD 64188.30 56541.43 – just a short distance to the east of the Whitendale Hanging Stones – has been declared by the Ordnance Survey to be the 'centre of Britain' is recounted on pages 67–9.

▶ Continue beside the boundary fence, through wet and boggy

▶ Map continues north on page 74

73

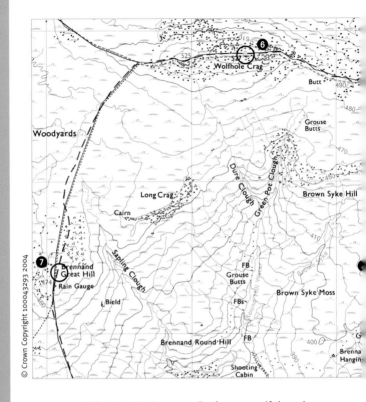

© Crown Copyright 1000043293 2004

country, to White Crag. Finally, the wall bends again and you arrive at the trig point at Wolfstone Crag ❻.

■ Wolfstone Crag, at 1729 ft (527 m), offers fine views down towards Penyghent, Ingleborough and Whernside, the Three Peaks of Yorkshire.

Further away, if there is adequate visibility, can be seen the Howgills and the Lake District fells.

The main rock at Wolfstone Crag has an interesting pattern of cups and grooves, which superficially resembles the prehistoric carvings to be found on similar millstone

fells have been so little explored in recent times that there may be discoveries waiting to be made by eagle-eyed walkers.

It is impossible to be unaware that walkers on the moors near Wolfhole Crag have company – the noisy and, in the nesting season, intimidating presence of lesser black-backed gulls.

▶ Continue beyond Wolfhole Crag, turning left by a stile to follow the rough path (previously opened as a concessionary route) signposted to Miller's House. This follows another boundary fence, and is quite difficult going. The next landmark of any note is Brennand Great Hill ❼.

■ Brennand Great Hill was the unlikely setting for a demonstration held on Forbidden Britain Day in September 1992, to protest at the lack of access to much of Bowland and in particular to most of the Abbeystead estate. About 250 people made their wet way here to hear speeches from, among

grit rocks on Ilkley Moor, about 30 miles (50 km) away to the east – though the more prosaic explanation is that the markings are simply the result of erosion. Lancashire County Archaeological Service is unaware of any carved stones in Bowland. Nevertheless, the Bowland others, Benny Rothman, the veteran leader of the 1932 Kinder Scout mass trespass. Chris Smith MP, at that stage Labour's shadow secretary of state for the environment (later a member of the first Blair cabinet and later still President of the Ramblers' Association), was also there. He talked of the importance of increasing formal access agreements, but made a prescient comment: 'The big task is when there won't be any need for access agreements at all, because there will be an automatic right of access throughout. That's what we need to aim for.'

▶ Continue from Brennand Great Hill past the rock outcrop known as Miller's House. At an appropriate time, cross to the eastern side of the fence. Beyond Miller's House, the path reaches the dark waters of Brennand Tarn ❽.

■ John Dixon in his engaging book of family walks *Dunsop*

Bridge, Bowland Forest brings his readers this way, too. Brennand Tarn hides a secret, he says: 'In the depths of these brackish waters is where the monks of Whalley Abbey hid their gold and silver plate from

the greedy hands of King Henry VIII'.

The county archaeological service in Preston knows of no such story, of course. But this is such an implausible tale that it really deserves to be true.

▶ From Brennand Tarn continue beside the boundary fence down, and then up, towards Whins Brow **9**. Visit the trig point, and then return back down the fence boundary to arrive at the Trough of Bowland road, at the walk's starting point.

A prominent rock at Wolfhole Crag

The Romans in Bowland

Anyone travelling up the motorway from Manchester to Carlisle passes within four miles (six and a half kilometres) of the trig point on the summit of Clougha fell, although most motorists don't notice as the Bowland hills pass them by. More than 1900 years before the M61 and the M6 were built, the Romans also needed to travel between Manchester and Carlisle (or, as they would have put it, between Mamucium and Luguvalium). The route their engineers planned for their arterial road north went straight through one of the wildest parts of the Forest of Bowland.

The route of the Romans' road north of the Ribble can be traced almost all the way on modern Ordnance Survey maps of the Bowland area. For most of the way, the dotted line on the map crosses fields and woods, away from modern roads. Close to Slaidburn, however, where the Roman road made a sharp turn to the north-west, the exact route of the road can be followed easily for a little more than three miles (five kilometres) across Croasdale Fell on the track known locally as the Hornby road.

This is the place where visitors to Bowland (including any who undertake Walk 7) meet the Roman road at first hand. It is, as Philip Graystone has said, a particularly spectacular section of the route.

Philip Graystone, a former headteacher from Blackburn, spent by his own reckoning more than thirty years getting to know the Roman road well, carefully following its route on the ground and noting what evidence remains today of its progress. His account *Walking Roman Roads in Bowland* is a fascinating introduction to the road (the book, originally published by the Centre for North-West Regional Studies at the University of Lancaster, is now sadly out of print but can be found in major libraries).

Graystone suggests that the scenery encountered by Romans as they travelled across what is now Croasdale Fell would have been very similar to that encountered by walkers today, with 'the same expanses of peat and bog, always wet with the frequent rainfall and poor drainage; the same heather and cotton grass; the same snow-covered landscape in winter'. What might have been different was the wildlife to be found: 'wild boar, and perhaps wolves, and even possibly the occasional bear'.

He continues: 'This must have been a difficult and, no doubt, unpopular route with the Roman soldiers, especially in winter. Nevertheless, given the necessity of crossing the Bowland Fells, the route chosen by the engineers showed great skill in avoiding the impassable river valleys and in keeping the really mountainous sections to a minimum . . . In its three-mile moorland journey from Low Fell to the next turn near Botton Head, the road runs parallel to the contours with almost uncanny regularity, instead of crossing them which would, of course, have meant ascent and descent.'

Roman roads were built initially for military purposes. The road through Bowland is part of a longer route which linked Chester (Deva) with Carlisle, passing through Northwich (Condate), Manchester, Ribchester (Bremetennacum), Burrow in Lonsdale (Calacum) and Brougham (Brocavum) on its way north. It was built in the second half of the first century AD, probably some time in the twenty years after AD 70. This was the time when first Cerealis and then Agricola were consolidating the Roman hold on northern England. The main British tribe in northern England, the Brigantes, had initially been prepared to accept Roman suzerainty, but by AD 69 had begun to change their minds.

From Manchester to Ribchester the road follows, in best Roman fashion, an almost straight line. In the Bowland section between Ribchester and Burrow in Lonsdale, however, the route includes a number of significant realignments, most notably at

Jeffrey Hill near Longridge, at the start of the Croasdale Fell section near Slaidburn and a third time at the summit a few miles later on Botton Head Fell. Once built, the road would have been used regularly for over 300 years, until the Romans left Britain for good in the early fifth century and the road entered a long twilight period.

The Hornby road over Croasdale Fell offers us the chance to walk where, once, the Romans walked too but there can be an initial sense of disappointment for modern visitors that the original appearance of the Roman road is not there to be appreciated. The Hornby road, although not tarmacked, has been resurfaced repeatedly in recent years with ballast, hard core and chippings. The original stone-built Roman road, if it still exists, lies out of reach below all this.

But in recent years an enthusiastic archaeology student, John Howard, has found a way which – just possibly – may allow visitors today to admire the road-building skills of the Roman engineers. He has discovered that, underneath the Hornby road, are no less than thirty-three stone culverts which were built to carry water under the road. As he has written: 'It is difficult to imagine that no interest has hitherto been taken in these interesting features, but perhaps there are few people who take pleasure in poking their heads down drains and other holes in the grounds! It is easy to miss, however, something that lies directly under a road you are walking along, and it is perhaps for this very reason that these culverts have been ignored.'

While many of John Howard's thirty-three culverts took him considerable efforts to uncover, some are readily apparent to any who look. One particularly good example is easy to spot,

One of the culverts under the Roman road

because a tree is growing out of the culvert exit. According to Howard, 'The culverts were generally built with the largest, flattest flags acting as floors, in order to permit the smooth flow of water; the roofs are invariably a series of long bridging capstones placed side by side across the width of the tunnels, and the sides were built from variously sized and shaped pieces of stone, apparently dry constructed but generally well put together.'

The issue, of course, is whether these culverts really are original Roman work, or simply engineering works undertaken in relatively modern times. John Howard accepts that the case is not yet proved, but nevertheless presents a good argument for them being original: he points out that culverts would have been needed for the original road, which was built to a high standard. Some culverts are deep below ground, deep enough surely to have been beyond the attention of later road improvers, while 'the very durability of the culverts bears witness to their strength of construction, which has only been seriously compromised in recent times by the coming of motor vehicles.' What might prove the Roman culvert theory would be the discovery of culverts of a similar design elsewhere on the Roman road, and at present much more research in this area is needed.

Whether these culverts are Roman or not is an interesting issue for walkers to ponder as they walk the Hornby road. In any case their discovery is a good example of the important role which keen observation can play in discovering more of Britain's past.

WALK 7

WHITENDALE AND THE ROMAN ROAD

DIFFICULTY 👟 👟   **DISTANCE** 11½ miles (18.5 km)

SLAIDBURN   BURN FELL   WHITENDALE   HORNBY ROAD   CROASDALE   SLAIDBURN

MAP OS Explorer OL41, Forest of Bowland

STARTING POINT Slaidburn village

PARKING The main car park for visitors is on the east side of Slaidburn, down by the River Hodder (GR 714524). Limited parking may be possible at the moor gate at the start of the Hornby road (GR 693549), reducing the distance of the walk by about 4 miles (6.4 km).

PUBLIC TRANSPORT Slaidburn is at the time of writing served by several buses a day (route B10) from Clitheroe and Settle. See page 66.

To the wild Whitendale valley and the Roman road.

■ Slaidburn is an attractive place to start and finish a walk, and a village trail booklet has been produced for visitors with time to explore the village properly.

The booklet is available at the Heritage Centre, which is itself worth a visit. One of the most interesting exhibits is a carved stone, the Angel Stone of Slaidburn, which was found locally and is believed to be pre-Norman Conquest.

Buildings of note in Slaidburn include St Andrew's

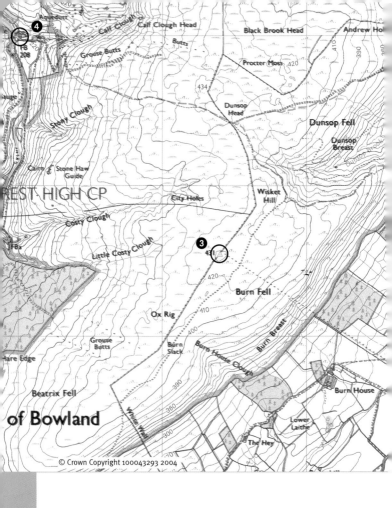

© Crown Copyright 100043293 2004

parish church, dating from about 1150, and Brennand's Endowed School, founded in 1717 to educate local boys using an endowment made in the will of John Brennand. This fine building is still the local primary school.

Many visitors are also likely to visit Slaidburn's pub, the

▶ Map continues northwards on pages 86–7

Hark to Bounty, originally known as the Dog Inn. The story of how it came by its present name is well known, if somewhat apocryphal: a

Victorian clergyman heard the sound of a favourite hound barking and exclaimed 'Just hark to Bounty'. The inn is one of the oldest buildings in

Slaidburn, dating from the sixteenth century. Upstairs is the old Forest court room where offences against the Forest laws were heard.

▶ From the Hark to Bounty, walk out of Slaidburn on the road heading west. After a little over a mile (1.6 km), continue as the road bends left, and almost

immediately take the tarmac drive to Burn Side **1**. The bridleway skirts the building and heads up to the moor edge.

At this point **2**, some people may choose to turn left along the moor edge wall, before heading up the side of Burn Fell to the trig point on the top. Encroaching bracken makes this a difficult task in high summer, however. The suggested route is to remain on the bridleway as it loops its way up above the valley of Dunsop Brook. For those keen not to miss the trig point ❸, a track along the upper wall at Wisket Hill offers easy walking.

■ The trig point at Burn Fell offers pleasant views of Stocks reservoir, and further afield to Easington Fell and Pendle Hill.

John Dixon, author of *Dunsop Bridge, Bowland Forest*, tells his readers of the crash of a USAF Flying Fortress bomber on the side of Burn Fell, on a flight in January 1945. According to Dixon, some parts of the aircraft wreckage remain scattered over this fell.

▶ Continue on the bridleway over Dunsop Head, heading down to the settlement at Whitendale ❹.

Pass the houses at Whitendale, and carry on along the track which heads northwards up the side of the Whitendale valley. The track becomes a rough and wet

footpath, making its way across the wild expanse of Whitendale Fell. After almost 2 miles (3 km), the path emerges on to the Hornby Road track ❺.

■ Somewhere in this area was a medieval cross, the

Whitendale Cross, a landmark which at one time rivalled in size the Cross of Greet, a few miles to the north-east.

History here, however, goes back considerably further, for the Hornby road at this point follows the route of the Roman road from Ribchester north, to the fort at Burrow-in-Lonsdale and eventually to Carlisle (see pages 78–82). The route deviates north from the Hornby road about a mile (1.6 km) beyond the point

The Roman road

where the Whitendale footpath comes in, at the watershed which previously marked the Yorkshire/ Lancashire county boundary.

The Hornby road is also known as the Salt Way or Salters Way Road, which most authors assume is a sign of the importance which the route once had for packhorse trains bringing salt from Morecambe Bay. Similar 'Salters Gate' packhorse routes are a feature in the south Pennines area. However, this may be an erroneous interpretation. In a recent journal article the historian Mary Higham comes up with another explanation: that Salter is an Anglicization of the Latin word *saltatorium*, and that it refers to a deer leap on the edge of the medieval hunting area. (As Latin scholars will know, the past participle of the verb *salio* – to leap – is *saltum*, from which comes the English technical term saltatorial, used to describe the way some animals jump.) High and Low Salter would have

been at the northern edge of the demarcated forest area.

▶ Turn right and follow the Hornby road back across Croasdale Fell. After a couple of miles (3 km), there is a choice of routes back to Slaidburn: one is to take the footpath which heads off down to Croasdale Brook, and then skirts Croasdale House and Shay House before emerging just to the north of Slaidburn village. This path is relatively well waymarked and avoids road walking.

The other route is to continue on the course of the Roman road until you reach the moor end and the Roman road route disappears off to the south near Burn Side ❻. Follow the tarmac road past Higher Wood House and Lanshaw. Near the turn to Myttons, the base of another ancient cross, Cross of Brown, can be found on the verge. From the craft centre at Myttons, it's worth taking the pleasant field footpath which skirts the side of Croasdale brook; after a stretch of woodland walking, the path emerges beside the health centre close to the centre of Slaidburn village.

Hen harriers

If there is one bird which symbolizes the Forest of Bowland, it is the hen harrier. This fine creature is one of Britain's less well-known birds of prey, though visitors will be able to mug up on its appearance from the official Bowland logo used on maps and guides or indeed from the road signs erected on approaches to the area. Seeing hen harriers in the flesh may not be quite so easy, though anyone observant who follows all the Bowland walks in this book has a strong likelihood of a sighting.

The hen harrier has had a tough time over the past century, and the reason is almost entirely human interference and persecution. One of the hen harrier's problems has been the fact that it is partial to, among other things, a plump little grouse chick. As a consequence, some gamekeepers on grouse moors in the past waged an unrelenting (but at that time legal) war, destroying nests and eggs and shooting or poisoning the birds. Numbers dropped so low, particularly in England and Wales, that the bird was in danger of disappearing altogether.

The hen harrier likes deep old heather, where it can nest undisturbed. According to one study, there are sufficient areas of habitat like this in England for perhaps 200–250 breeding pairs. In fact, each year there are only about 10–20 pairs nesting in England, and by far the most important breeding area in England is the Forest of Bowland.

Not surprisingly, English Nature and the RSPB are concerned to protect Bowland's hen harriers as best they can. Although resources are not available for the sort of round-the-clock surveillance of nests undertaken for some osprey or golden eagle nests, a close watch is kept on the nests during the breeding season. Typically, the birds will move into their nesting territory in March, laying eggs from perhaps the second week in April. Incubation lasts four or five weeks before the hen harrier chicks are hatched. Then follows a period of another five or six weeks before the young birds are fledged. However, the breeding season can be affected by the weather: heavy rains at the wrong time in the breeding cycle can have a serious effect on the number of chicks successfully raised.

Hen harriers are particularly agile and acrobatic flyers. The bird's most distinctive trait is its ability to swoop very low over

Hen harrier

the ground, often taking prey before the prey is aware it is about to be taken (as well as grouse chicks, the hen harrier takes other small birds and small mammals). The male bird also has a particularly fine mating display, which has given the hen harrier the nickname of 'skydancer'. The bird tries to impress its mate by performing spectacular aeronautical displays, rising hundreds of feet and then tumbling towards the earth.

Hen harriers, like other birds of prey, are now fully protected by the law. It is a criminal offence to intentionally kill or injure a bird, take or destroy eggs or damage nests. It is also an offence under English law to 'intentionally or recklessly' disturb the hen harrier while it is building a nest or incubating eggs.

Reputable shooting estates and their keepers have put the dodgy practices of the past behind them. However the RSPB believes that the hen harrier is still facing persecution, perhaps from rogue elements in the gamekeeper fraternity. In 2003, the police identified a 'real and imminent threat' facing hen harriers, and decided to launch the national Operation Artemis, targeting criminals involved in persecution of the bird. A dedicated website www.savethehenharrier.com was launched to help promote the campaign.

Hen harriers are more widespread north of the border, with between 360 and 500 pairs breeding in Scotland each year. However, the police are concerned that in Scotland too the bird is at risk from persecution, including poisoning.

Even if the hen harrier is Bowland's honorary mascot, it is not the only important species of bird to nest here. Peregrine falcons also breed in the area, as does the relatively rare short-eared owl. Another bird to look out for is the merlin, Britain's smallest bird of prey.

Slaidburn

It sounds like an implausible pub quiz question: What links the quiet Bowland village of Slaidburn with the film *The Full Monty*?

The answer is the brass band tune entitled 'Slaidburn' which plays its part in almost the first scene of the movie. Those who have seen the film will recall the moment when the Sheffield works band march their way through a derelict steel works, interrupting a little petty larceny from Robert Carlyle's character Gaz. And the tune they play as they march will be instantly recognizable to almost any brass band player.

'Slaidburn' was written by William Rimmer in the early years of the twentieth century, after he had visited the village and been pressed to conduct the Slaidburn Silver Band. The band members surely couldn't have believed their luck: at the time Rimmer was perhaps the greatest name in the brass band world. Born in Southport in 1862, he conducted some of the most successful bands of the day and also composed or arranged many of the most popular tunes.

The story goes that he was in Slaidburn on what was supposed to be a restful holiday after ill health, but couldn't resist the opportunity to help the local village band improve their performance. With his help, this is just what they did. Afterwards the players asked him to compose a march for them to play, and 'Slaidburn' was the result.

Slaidburn Silver Band is still going strong today, more than a century after it was started. Its current conductor John Cowking, the third generation of his family to be involved in the band, says that the tune's fame regularly brings players from other bands to Bowland, fired with the desire to play 'Slaidburn' with the Slaidburn band. The Silver Band does, of course, play a host of other material; but it is clear that William Rimmer's tribute to his time in the village is going to stay in the repertoire for a very long time to come.

WALK 8

ROEBURNDALE

DIFFICULTY 👢 👢   **DISTANCE** 7 miles (11.3 km)

| ROEBURNDALE (MIDDLE WOOD) | HARTERBECK | GOODBER COMMON | OUTHWAITE | ROEBURNDALE |

MAP OS Explorer OL41, Forest of Bowland

STARTING POINT On the no-through-road from Hornby and Wray to High Salter, near Back Farm (GR 600652)

PARKING Verge parking is possible at places on the Roeburndale road, but take care not to block farm gates or drives. One possible place to park is just south of the junction of the Hornby and Wray roads (GR 599659).

PUBLIC TRANSPORT Occasional buses on service 80/80A (Mon–Sat) run from Lancaster and Ingleton to Wray village, about 1¾ miles (2.8 km) from the start of the walk.

This lower-level route includes fine woodland walking in the Roeburn valley, as well as a mile (1.6 km) of open moorland on Goodber Common.

▶ From the road to High Salter follow the right of way to Back Farm, and then continue through fields and woods as the path drops down the hillside. The footpath turns left to cross a field towards the buildings of Middle Wood.

■ Middle Wood is an environmental centre which specializes in ecological

buildings, sustainability and alternative energy. The centre operates a charitable trust which, among other things, organizes study weekends and longer courses in topics such as permaculture (managing the land in a sustainable way) and straw bale building. Middle Wood

© Crown Copyright 100043293 2004

itself runs an organic farm and operates as an informal community, which is home to a number of families and individuals.

The turf-covered building approached by the footpath is Middle Wood's study centre, complete with meeting room, kitchen and two dormitories. Wind and passive solar power help to heat it, while extra insulation has been provided by using sheep's wool. Next door is the 'community yurt', based on the traditional Mongolian yurt design. It serves as a gathering place for Middle Wood residents and visitors.

▶ Having passed the study centre, follow a track down the hill for a short way. As the track bends to the right continue ahead, following the waymarks. Steep steps lead to a small wooden bridge crossing over the River Roeburn ❶.

■ The Roeburn is one of Bowland's most delightful rivers, and the valley is normally a quiet peaceful place. Very occasionally, however, another side of the river's character is shown. In August 1967 the Roeburn turned into a fierce torrent, after heavy rain had fallen higher up on the moors. Flash flooding swept away bridges and severely damaged cottages in Wray.

▶ Cross the footbridge and the field beyond, turning left at the end into the woods to briefly head north. After about 200 yards (200 m), turn right along a concessionary footpath. This runs back in a southerly direction through the Roeburndale Woods, climbing gradually.

■ This woodland is an important habitat and part has been formally designated a Site of Special Scientific Interest. According to the Middle Wood centre, the woods were historically managed with a regular coppicing programme, with the timber and scrub used, among other things, for charcoal, oak baskets, Lancashire clogs and besom brushes. Middle Wood is now once again trying to manage the woods, with the wood being used for a variety of purposes, including the creation of rustic furniture.

Below the woods, in a bend in the river, is the Roeburndale camping barn, also operated by the Middle Wood centre.

▶ Continue along the concessionary footpath, ignoring the wider forestry tracks. The path can be overrun by bracken in summer.

After a mile (1.6 km) or so, the path begins to drop. When another waymarked concessionary path comes in from the left, take this to climb once more towards the edge of the woods.

After a short distance, the path reaches the edge of the woods, by an old metal gate ❷. Cross through here to the rough pastureland beyond, climbing up the hillside with a wall to your right and a little clough to your left. Shortly, find the stone stile in the wall. Cross this stile, to pick up the right of way. At a

stone barn, turn half-left to follow the footpath to Harterbeck Farm.

At Harterbeck, follow waymarks to the left-hand side of the farm, to find the right of way heading south to Goodber Beck ❸.

■ It is worth crossing the footbridge over Goodber Beck to have a closer look at the waterfall here. The water falls about 35 ft (10 m) into a pool at the head of a small ravine. The falls, modest when the river is low, are more impressive after rain.

To reach the top of the falls, clamber over the rocks beside the river immediately after crossing the footbridge.

Roeburndale

▶ Cross back over the footbridge (or, of course, choose not to cross at all) and walk through the meadow, keeping Goodber Beck on your right. At the end of the field, a gate leads to the open moorland of Goodber Common **4**. Turn left, to pick up one of the sheep trods which head off parallel to the moorside wall.

In comparison with other moorland areas of Bowland, Goodber Common is both dry and easy walking. Keep the moorside wall to your left, enjoying the views ahead of the valley of Wenningdale and the Three Peaks beyond.

After just over a mile (1.6 km), the moor wall bends to the left, to approach the farmhouse of Scale **5**. Leave the access land beside Hunt's Gill Beck, and make your way to the minor road.

■ This area was the scene of considerable coal-mining activity in the late eighteenth and nineteenth centuries, with a particularly important mine at Smeer Hall just to the north of Scale. Some of the disused coal shafts (which might have been as much as 150 ft/45 m deep) are still marked on modern OS maps.

Coal was also mined in other parts of Bowland, including Littledale, Quernmore and Fell End, west of Clougha.

▶ Cross to the site of Wray Wood Moor Tarn **6** (now unfortunately dried up), and pick up the field footpath which runs north-westwards close to Outhwaite.

■ Outhwaite (the local pronunciation is something approximating to 'u-thit') is a settlement with the Scandinavian -thwaite suffix, suggesting a settlement that was here in Viking times. The farm and surrounding buildings date back to the seventeenth century; however, some of the timber used in the present buildings is older.

▶ After about ½ mile (0.8 km), turn left on to another footpath, heading across fields back down into the Roeburn valley. Pick up the footpath over the river and past Middle Wood centre, back to the walk's starting point.

Raven Castle

As anyone who undertakes Walk 9 in this book will discover, the small cluster of rocks in the moors six miles (ten kilometres) or so north of Slaidburn bears the name of Raven's Castle. Apart from helping to demarcate the old Lancashire/Yorkshire border, its role in history seems exceptionally modest.

It was here, however, that the nineteenth-century writer John Roby chose to set one of his 'traditional' Lancashire folk tales, a tale of evil designs and dark deeds in a bleak moorland setting which – against all the odds – nevertheless manages to have a happy ending.

The story appears in *Traditions of Lancashire*, published in 1829, in the period when Sir Walter Scott's historical novels were much in fashion. Like Scott (who read and praised *Traditions of Lancashire*), Roby dug deep into all kinds of local historical myths and legends to weave his tales – what he called 'the more entertaining, though sometimes apocryphal, narratives which exemplify and embellish the records of our forefathers'.

Roby sets 'Raven Castle' in the seventeenth century. The opening paragraph gives a sense of what is to follow:

Situated amid the wild and high moorlands, at whose feet hath stood for ages the royal and ducal capital of the county palatine of Lancaster, once rose a strong border defence called Raven Castle. Its site only remains. This noble and castellated fortress now lies an almost undistinguishable heap on the barren moor; the sheep browse above it, and the herdsman makes his pillow where warriors and dames once met in chivalric pomp, and the chieftain held his feudal and barbaric court.

Raven Castle, Roby envisages, is a dark and well-fortified mansion complete with everything that the best medieval castle should have: a moat and bridge, a courtyard, a gallery, turrets and battlements, narrow winding staircases leading to numerous chambers, and – so it seems – the ghost of Lady Fairfax, who has recently drowned herself having heard of the death of her husband Sir Henry on the battlefields of Germany.

The tale opens as two dubious characters, Michael and Anthony, are riding through the Trough of Bowland, through 'the almost pathless wilds of the forest' on their way to Raven Castle, where they have been summonsed by Sir Henry's private secretary Hildebrand Wentworth. With both Sir Henry and his wife dead, only their orphaned children stand between Hildebrand and the Fairfax fortune. Michael and Anthony may be able to help him, therefore, with a little task . . .

The children, a boy aged four or five and his younger sister, are drawn away from their weeping nurse and given to the care of the two horsemen. Hildebrand Wentworth's plan, we quickly learn, is for the children to be taken into Yorkshire, to the falls near Ingleton. Here the riders with their charges dismount, for a 'rest':

The roar of the torrent grew louder. Suddenly they entered upon a sort of irregular amphitheatre – woods rising above each other to the very summit of the hills by which they were surrounded. A swollen waterfall was visible, below which a bare and flattened trunk, whose boughs had apparently been but just lopped, was thrown across the torrent. A ruined keep or donjon was seen above a line of dark firs, crowning the summit of a steep crag that rose abruptly from the river.

Anthony, who has been frightened by the appearance of Lady Fairfax's ghost and is already repenting of his involvement, is all too aware of what Michael is planning to do. The two men quarrel and fight. After a desperate hand-to-hand tussle at the edge of the falls, Michael's hold on the tree trunk is loosened: 'One startling plunge, and the wretch sank in the rolling waters. An agonising yell, and but one, escaped him, as he hung quivering over that yawning portal to eternity; the next cry was choked by the seethe of the boiling foam.'

The children have been saved. Meanwhile, back at Raven Castle and ignorant of developments at Ingleton, Hildebrand Wentworth is ready to reap the fruits of his villainy. But all is not going well. Hildebrand is 'restless and oppressed by undefined and terrible apprehensions', which are only reinforced when a mysterious messenger arrives from the wars in Europe. Sir Henry Fairfax, it transpires, is not dead at all but is being held prisoner near the Rhine.

Time passes. High up on the Bowland fells, Hildebrand Wentworth takes to pacing the rooms of Raven Castle:

From a ruined doorway he ascended a narrow stair, and had penetrated far into the interior of that part of the castle which, in some measure, remained entire, when, for the first time, he seemed startled into a consciousness of his situation. It was an appalling scene of solitude and decay . . . Narrow streams of light flitted across the dense vapours, visible only in their gleam. Involuntarily did Hildebrand pass on: impelled by some unseen but resistless power, he durst not retrace his footsteps.

And here, in the Raven Castle gallery, he catches sight of a female figure, loosely wrapped in a dark cloak. It must be the ghost of Lady Fairfax, ready to curse and damn Hildebrand to hell. Hildebrand rushes away, but as he leaves the castle beside the bridge over the moat, he is immediately confronted by Sir Henry, released from his prison ordeal and back to claim what is rightfully his. Hildebrand, trapped, has only one option: 'he rushed towards the bridge, and, ere his purpose could be anticipated, with one wild yell, precipitated himself into the waters.'

Wicked Hildebrand Wentworth is no more. But there is a final twist to the tale: Lady Fairfax, aware of his plotting, had – so we discover – faked her own death and remained at Raven Castle acting the role of ghost. Husband, wife and children are happily reunited: joy, we are told, attended them through the remainder of their earthly careers.

As may be deduced, John Roby spins some good Gothic yarns. His book has become something of a classic and has recently been brought back into print, in two volumes, by an enterprising bookseller in Bury.

WALK 9

RAVEN'S CASTLE

DIFFICULTY 👢 👢 **DISTANCE 7 miles (11.3 km)**

CROSS OF GREET BRIDGE — CATLOW — BOWLAND KNOTTS — COLD STONE — RAVEN'S CASTLE — CROSS OF GREET — CROSS OF GREET BRIDGE

MAP OS Explorer OL41, Forest of Bowland

STARTING POINT Cross of Greet Bridge, on Slaidburn – Bentham road (GR 702590)

PARKING Parking is available at the bridge for about six cars.

PUBLIC TRANSPORT See page 66

Magnificent views to the Three Peaks and beyond. This walk is generally on paths and tracks, but includes a little rough moorland walking. The route will be damp under foot in places.

▶ Leave the Cross of Greet Bridge by the footpath which runs alongside the juvenile River Hodder. The first ½ mile (0.8 km) can be boggy.

Follow the path as it turns away from the river up the hill near Catlow Farm, to cross into a pasture. Continue on the right of way past the prominent barn above Catlow ❶, initially following a drainage channel. When the channel bends round to the right, continue north-eastwards to the hill top.

■ To your right are views down to Stocks reservoir. Stocks is a relatively recent addition to the landscape, built in the 1920s in order to supply water to the people of Blackpool and the neighbouring Fylde region. Its construction involved the destruction of the village of Stocks-in-Bowland, including a church, the Travellers Rest pub and a primary school, the remains of which now lie beneath the water. The stone from the church was later

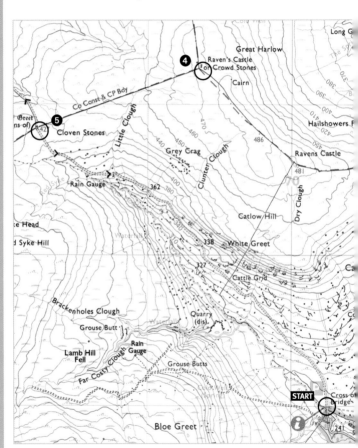

used to build a small chapel on the eastern shore.

As with other reservoirs, the work of building Stocks involved the creation of a temporary settlement, complete with cinema and other amenities, to house the several hundred workers required. The reservoir was completed and given a formal royal opening in 1932.

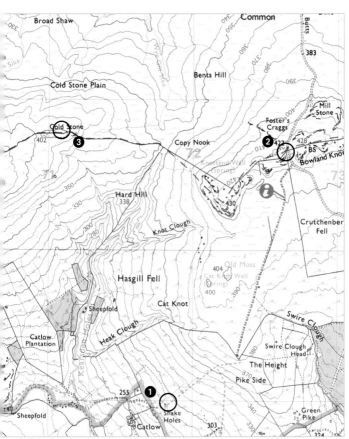

▶ At the hill top, find the track which runs down the further side of the moor, to the left of a stone wall. The track makes straight for the outcrop of rocks at Bowland Knotts ❷.

■ Bowland Knotts make up one of the more impressive gritstone outcrops in the Forest of Bowland, and it can be worth taking a little time to explore the rocks. This is a popular place for motorists to park to enjoy the views.

▶ Turn left at Bowland Knotts, to pick up the grassy path which runs beside (and to the north of) the boundary wall. This drops down to the Kearsden Holes valley at Copy Nook, before climbing again to the Cold Stones. By Bowland standards, this is relatively easy walking on dryish ground.

■ The delight of this ridge walk ❸ is the view which – weather permitting – can be enjoyed across to the Yorkshire Dales to the north. In particular, this is one of the best places to come

to admire the Three Peaks: Penyghent to the right, flat-topped Ingleborough ahead, and Whernside (the highest of the three at 2415 ft/ 736 m) a little way behind Ingleborough. As the walk progresses, the view of these peaks, and the relationship

between them, subtly changes. Also in the picture should be Great Whernside (to the right of Penyghent) and Gragareth and the Leck Fell ridge (to the left of Ingleborough). Further away, but visible in fine weather, are the Howgill fells and the mountains of the Lake District.

▶ Continue on the grassy track beside the wall. The destination is Raven's Castle. Confusingly there are two places on OS maps with this name, one with an apostrophe and one without.

Sykes Farm, Trough of Bowland

The suggested route for the walk continues past a small cairn to the second, apostrophed, Raven's Castle ❹. (The walk could be cut short by following the wall down across Catlow Hill from the first Ravens Castle, but this involves a steep descent.)

■ A small outcrop of rocks at Raven's Castle bears the name of Crowd Stones. This is presumably the location which John Roby had in mind for the dramatic goings-on and dark deeds he recounted in his *Traditions of Lancashire* (see page 101).

▶ Cross over the boundary fence, and follow the wall westwards to reach the site of the Cross of Greet, on the Slaidburn–Bentham road ❺.

■ Unfortunately only the stump of the Cross of Greet remains, showing the socket in which the main shaft of the cross used to be fitted. The cross, which is believed to be of monastic origin, must once have been an imposing sight.

The Cross of Greet marked for centuries the boundary between Lancashire and Yorkshire. It was only local government reorganization in 1974 which transferred the land south of here from the West Riding into Lancashire.

▶ From here, there is 1$\frac{1}{2}$ miles (2.5 km) of road walking, back to the starting point. The good news, however, is that the walk is downhill all the way.

■ As you drop towards Cross of Greet Bridge, the track of the industrial railway can be seen on the opposite side of the River Hodder valley. The railway was built for Stocks reservoir to convey stone which was quarried near by.

A vision on Pendle Hill

There are many reasons to climb to the top of Pendle Hill, and different rewards and satisfactions when the climb is successfully achieved – depending of course on the weather and, perhaps, the mood of the walker. But few people have the experience on Pendle which came to George Fox, when he reached the summit on a day in 1652.

For Fox, Pendle Hill turned out to be a place of vision, a vision which changed his life and that of many people who came after him. Fired by this experience, Fox went on to found the Religious Society of Friends, better known as the Quakers.

George Fox was born in 1624, which meant that he was a young man in his twenties when England went through one of the most turbulent and revolutionary periods in its history. The story of the battles between Charles I and Parliament, the civil war and the eventual execution of the king in 1649 is likely to be familiar from school history, but what may perhaps be less well known is the ferment of ideas which swept the country during the period. This was a time when, in both politics and religion, established ideas were up for question and for often fiery debate. It was a time when the Establishment, including the Church, came under intense scrutiny and attack.

George Fox was one of a significant number of people who were then travelling the country in order to criticize the established Church and its priests, and to preach an alternative Christian message which they claimed was closer to the original ideas of Jesus. Fox began his spiritual quest in 1643 when he was nineteen, leaving his home county of Leicestershire to travel across southern England and the Midlands. He came to the view that, as he put it, 'being bred at Oxford or Cambridge was not enough to fit and qualify men to be ministers of Christ'. Everyone, he felt, could be enlightened by 'the divine light'.

By the early 1650s, Fox was travelling widely as an itinerant preacher. In 1652 he had visited various towns in west Yorkshire and Derbyshire, before crossing into Lancashire. 'As we went,' he recorded in his journal, 'I spied a great high hill called Pendle Hill . . . I was moved of the Lord to go atop of it.' This he achieved, although not without some apparent difficulty ('it was so steep'). His journal continues: 'And when I came atop of it I saw Lancashire sea; and there atop of the hill I was moved to sound the day of the Lord; and the Lord let me see a-top of the hill in what places he had a great people to be gathered.'

The task, as Fox saw it, was to help gather this 'great people' and this he rapidly set about doing. Many parts of the north of England, including several areas in Bowland, became strong Quaker centres. However, while his message was to attract some, it was also to lead to much persecution and ridicule.

Unlike other religious sects which were established in the seventeenth century, Quakerism put down deep roots and now has practising adherents in over fifty countries. Because of George Fox's vision, Pendle Hill remains something of a special place for many Quakers. It has also given its name to the Quaker college in Pennsylvania.

WALK 10

ROBIN HOOD'S WELL (PENDLE HILL)

DIFFICULTY  **DISTANCE 7¾ miles (12.5 km)**

WORSTON — MEARLEY HALL — PENDLE HILL (SCOUT CAIRN) — ROBIN HOOD'S WELL — HOOKCLIFFE — WORSTON

MAP OS Explorer OL41, Forest of Bowland. Also useful is the locally produced map, Paths Around Pendle (published by Duncan Armstrong, 01282 778591).

STARTING POINT Worston village, near Clitheroe

PARKING Park carefully in Worston village, near the Calf's Head pub (GR 769428).

PUBLIC TRANSPORT Clitheroe (2 miles/3 km) is served by trains from Manchester and Blackburn and by buses from Blackburn, Burnley, Skipton and other Lancashire towns. The nearest bus stop to Worston is about a mile (1.6 km) away, on Chatburn Road (currently served by local buses C2 and C3).

An airy walk on the 'other', quieter, side of Pendle Hill, offering fine views across to the Forest of Bowland and the Yorkshire Dales. Relatively easy walking.

■ The attractive village of Worston is particularly peaceful, in a no-through-road and cut off from the rest of Lancashire by the Clitheroe by-pass. Among the houses in the village is one with three stone heraldic shields over its porch, believed to

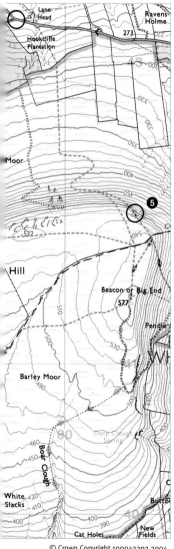

© Crown Copyright 100043293 2004

have been purloined from Sawley Abbey after the dissolution of the monasteries under Henry VIII.

Pendle Hill dominates the village, and Worston's location has in the past caused it problems: in 1669 a 'mighty torrent' of water unexpectedly emerged from the depths of the hill and raced down the hillside in a wave several feet high. The downstairs rooms of the houses in the village were inundated.

▶ Leave Worston, taking the field footpath behind the Calf's Head and heading south-eastwards towards Little Mearley Hall. Turn right on to the farm track.

■ From the track, the frontage of Little Mearley Hall ❶ is visible. This building dates back to the late sixteenth century, and has an interesting five-sided bay window much admired by Nikolaus Pevsner in his *Buildings of England* (he calls it 'gorgeous'). This building may also have acquired redundant stonework from nearby Sawley Abbey or Whalley Abbey.

▶ Keep on the track from Little Mearley Hall to Mearley Hall, and turn left past the farm buildings on the footpath up the hillside. Continue past the first barn ❷, but leave the footpath before it drops down to Howcroft Brook and Howcroft Barn. The aim is to look for a sheep trod which can take you round the end of Pendle Hill, through the bracken.

In due course, you should meet a much better-defined path running up from the Nick of Pendle road. Turn left on to this path, and follow it all the way to the cairn near the summit, on Mearley Moor ❸.

■ The cairn was erected by Clayton-le-Moors Harriers, a long-established local running club. Pendle Hill is a popular venue for fell races, the Tour of Pendle race held every autumn being the longest and most arduous. The race involves 17 miles (27 km) of running and 4250 ft (1300 m) of climbing. Another race, the Mearley Clough fell race, begins – like this walk – in Worston and involves a single ascent of the hill to the Scout cairn (see below), a climb of about 1200 ft (365 m). The winner usually manages to be back at the finish, near the Calf's Head pub, in just over thirty minutes.

Nevertheless, the Clayton-le-Moors cairn is a reminder of the risks of taking to the hills, commemorating two club members who died in accidents. The death of Judith Taylor, an experienced fell runner who was taking part, in near blizzard conditions, in the classic horseshoe Kentmere fell race in the Lake District on Easter Sunday 1994, cast a particular cloud over the close-knit fell-running community.

▶ The track continues along the ridge. Weather permitting, of course, this is a wonderful walk, with magnificent views to be enjoyed. Easington Fell is an obvious landmark across the

Ribble valley, with the hills of Bowland beyond: the round cone of Parlick is particularly easy to identify. Further to the south-west is the Ribble estuary and the sea near Southport. To the north are the Three Peaks, and other hills of the Yorkshire Dales.

Continue past the Scout cairn ❹, erected in 1982 to mark the seventy-fifth anniversary of the Scout movement. The cairn also commemorates two local Scout leaders.

The ridge walk passes a stone-built shelter, a convenient picnic site in poor weather, and arrives at a ladder stile. From here the path swings right, to arrive shortly at another ladder stile.

■ It is worth crossing over this stile, and walking the short distance to the trig point on Pendle Hill Big End. This is also visited in Walk 11 (see page 125).

▶ The route now heads from the stile straight down the hillside. It is tempting to hurry down the main path, as it disappears down towards the valley below. However, this involves missing one of the main attractions of the walk. Instead, search out the parallel path which runs some yards (metres) to the right, slightly lower down the hill. Soon you will hear running water and arrive at Robin Hood's Well ❺.

■ Ordnance Survey has done walkers a disservice by omitting to mark Robin Hood's Well (GR 805420) on its Explorer maps. Although so close to the main tourist area of Big End, it remains undiscovered by many who walk on the hill.

This is one of the few springs on Pendle, and its water has been enjoyed for centuries. George Fox, the founder of the Quaker movement (see pages 111–112), reports in his journal that 'as I went down, on the hillside I found a spring of water and refreshed myself, for I had eaten little and drunk little for several days,' and it is almost certain that it was this water he drank. Indeed, the spring has the alternative name of Fox's Well, in memory of his visit.

▶ page 120

The unmistakable shape of Pendle Hill

It's possible to drink from the spring water as it emerges directly from the hillside. However, it's perhaps more exciting to open the metal lid to find the 'well' below. Tied to the underneath of the lid and attached to a chain should be a cup, which can be used for dunking in the water. According to local stories, this is the best water in Lancashire.

Why should the spring carry the name of Robin Hood? The companion Freedom to Roam volume which covers the south Pennines explores the many references to Robin Hood place names in the north of England, and suggests that Nottinghamshire may not be the only county with a claim to Robin Hood's memory. However, it is also possible that the well's name alludes to the mischievous nature spirit Robin Goodfellow (turned by Shakespeare into the character Puck in *A Midsummer Night's Dream*), and that the well was significant in pagan times.

▶ At the bottom of the hill ➏, turn left on to the road and immediately left again, to take the concessionary footpath to Hookcliffe. From here take one of the field footpaths to Worsaw End, and find the footpath which skirts the south side of Worsaw Hill ➐.

■ Worsaw Hill is an interesting round hill, almost entirely made of limestone – in contrast to Pendle, which has a layer of hard millstone grit rock. (Worsaw Hill is not designated as access land.)

▶ Follow the field footpath back to the centre of Worston village.

WALK 11

PENDLE HILL BIG END

DIFFICULTY 👢 👢 **DISTANCE 10 miles (16 km)**

SABDEN DEERSTONES OGDEN CLOUGH PENDLE HILL BIG END BOAR CLOUGH OGDEN CLOUGH SPENCE MOOR CHURN CLOUGH SABDEN

MAPS Two OS Explorer maps are needed: OS Explorer 287, West Pennine Moors and either Explorer OL41, Forest of Bowland, or OL21, South Pennines. Also useful is the locally produced map, Paths Around Pendle (published by Duncan Armstrong, 01282 778591).

STARTING POINT Sabden village

PARKING Main car park in Sabden (opposite the White Hart pub (GR 780374)

PUBLIC TRANSPORT Buses run (approximately every two hours) from Clitheroe and Whalley, and from Padiham, Burnley and Colne. In addition, in recent years the 'Witch Hopper' bus has run on Sundays and Bank Holidays on a circular route around Pendle Hill (Burnley–Clitheroe–Nelson–Burnley).

A less well-walked route to the top of Pendle Hill. Some moorland walking.

■ Most people approach Pendle Hill either from Barley village or from the Nick of Pendle, where the road between Sabden and Clitheroe cuts through the hill ridge. This route offers a less familiar approach to the hill, starting in the village of Sabden and climbing up to

▶ page 124

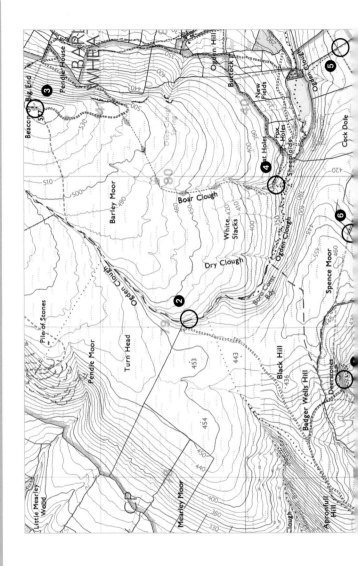

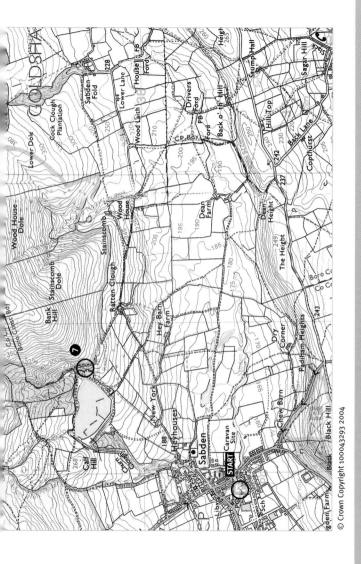

the open moors through attractive countryside. The destination, however, remains the ever-popular trig point on Pendle Hill Big End.

▶ Leave Sabden village, turning up towards the parish church at the Whalley Road crossroads. Turn left before the church and follow the road round to Badger Wells Cottages. Head up the well-walked footpath to the right of the cottages.

A pleasant path runs up the side of Badger Wells Water, round Calf Hill. When a track from the Trough of Bowland joins from the west, continue steadily climbing, skirting the wood above Churn Clough reservoir and heading towards the Deerstones outcrop of rocks. To reach the rocks themselves leave the main path shortly before a ladder stile.

■ If you have time to spare at the Deerstones, search for the Giant's Footprints (or perhaps they are the Devil's Footprints) ❶. These are two (roughly) foot-shaped marks, each over 2 ft (0.66 m) long.

One story is that the Devil was at the Deerstones picking up rocks to try to hurl at Clitheroe Castle.

▶ From the Deerstones, make your way across the open moorland of Black Hill, aiming north-eastwards, to pick up the track running from Nick of Pendle to Ogden Clough. (To avoid rough walking, it's possible to return to the ladder stile and follow the footpath back across Badger Wells Hill. This route is further, but may keep your feet drier.)

Turn right when you reach the well-walked track, and follow it as it bends round the northern side of Ogden Clough ❷.

■ At this point, according to Joe Bates, 'You are now in a part of Pendle where you feel a thousand miles from anywhere.' Joe Bates (or 'Boshmengro') published his book of *Rambles Twixt Pendle and Holme* in the late 1920s, when copies were on sale in local newsagents for sixpence. He waxes lyrical about the delights of walking in this area: 'Pendle is a tremendous hill, long, broad, and ponderous; full of lines, cracks, gullies, cloughs; exposing rocks, screes, precipices and slopes . . . There are waterfalls of grace and beauty; heather patches that glow a full ripe purple . . . there are sheaves of rushes, sweet, sappy and delicately tapering, and grass that is sea green in May, yet blushes red as the rose from December until Spring.' But Pendle can also, as he points out, be a place of sudden mists, of gales, and in winter of deep snowdrifts.

Joe Bates can be our guide for the next part of the walk: 'From here the clough bends round to the right; the stream narrows, the high banks creep closer in; peat banks and black peat gullies shew on the right; the pools are shallower, and the stream bottom covered in places with long tresses of algae.'

▶ Continue along the side of Ogden Clough for a mile (1.6 km) or so. Just past an old boundary stone, marked with the letters WA, cross the stream and take the concessionary footpath through a gate and up the side of Pendle. This next stretch of path has been carefully flagged.

You will emerge on to the summit plateau of Pendle Hill, just beside the trig point ❸.

■ This part of Pendle is known as both the Big End and Beacon, the latter name recalling the fact that the hill was historically used as a site for signal beacons. A particularly spectacular beacon was lit in the summer of 1883, to commemorate Queen Victoria's Jubilee. The beacon site, close to the trig point, is on what was originally a Bronze Age burial mound.

▶ Follow the main path south-west along the hill brow from the trig point, in due course taking a right-hand path which bears off to the west, towards the top of Boar Clough. Boar Clough is the official name shown on maps, but the clough is also known locally as Whimberry or Wimberry Clough. The footpath is well marked by cairns and by the occasional 'witch' signpost, showing that this is part of the route of the Pendle Way.

■ The Pendle Way is an enjoyable 45-mile (72-km) circular walk around the borough of Pendle. It was devised as the result of a suggestion by the Pendle Enterprise Trust in 1985, with construction work starting a year later. The route encircles the old mill towns of Nelson and Colne.

▶ At the bottom of Boar Clough ❹, you rejoin Ogden Clough. To follow the suggested route,

turn left to follow the clough down to the side of Upper Ogden reservoir. Alternatively, pick your way across the river and then climb steeply up the side of the clough, following the wall boundary, towards Cock Dole.

■ Both the Upper Ogden and Lower Ogden reservoirs provide drinking water for people in the Nelson area. Upper Ogden was the first to be completed, in 1906. When full, it is 58 ft (18 m) deep, and can hold about 54 million gallons of water.

▶ If you have followed the cloughside down to Upper Ogden reservoir, cross over the dam and follow the footpath straight up the hill beyond. Turn right at a meeting of paths ❺, and follow the footpath across Driver Height towards Spence Moor. Though a path is waymarked, be warned that it rapidly deteriorates as it approaches some quite boggy land. This stretch of moor is known as Stephenson Dole.

■ It is probably obligatory at this point to mention something about the 'Pendle witches' since 'Demdike' and her family, central figures in the 1612 witchcraft panic and trial, lived at the bottom of the hill near Sadler's Farm. Several others among those accused of witchcraft also lived very close by.

Looking up Ogden Clough

The story of the 'witches' of Pendle has developed an unstoppable momentum, and is now a major aspect of the local tourist industry. This interest is not just a modern phenomenon, however; it dates back at least to the middle of the nineteenth century when novelist William Harrison Ainsworth published his popular *The Lancashire Witches*, re-igniting interest in the story.

The events on which the story is based took place between March 1612, when Demdike's grand-daughter was accused of cursing a pedlar near Colne, and August 1612, when eight women and two men were found guilty at Lancaster of witchcraft and executed by hanging. The tale brings together on the one hand a zealous magistrate keen to curry favour at a time when the king was obsessed with witchcraft, and on the other a group of people almost all of whom were living in abject poverty and several of whom suffered from physical or mental disability (or both). Anti-Catholicism may also have played a part in bringing at least one so-called 'witch' to trial.

There is no shortage of publications which tell this tale in much more detail. For a dispassionate account Walter Bennett's pamphlet *The Pendle Witches*, first published in 1957 and since regularly reprinted, has much to recommend it.

▶ The footpath crosses a ladder stile ❻, heading back towards the Deerstones. For an alternative route back, however, turn left just before the stile and follow the wall boundary downhill. This is an attractive path, with fine views south across the valley to the Rossendale fells beyond. The path begins to descend rapidly, arriving eventually at Churn Clough reservoir ❼. From here turn left to follow the field footpath back past New York Farm to Sabden.

The Clarion House

The tea comes in generous pint-sized mugs, and there's no problem with eating your own sandwiches on the premises. But the Clarion House, tucked away in fields below Pendle Hill, is more than just a comfortable place where walkers and cyclists stop for a Sunday afternoon cuppa or a picnic. It is a survivor of a major movement in English social history.

In December 1891 the pioneering journalist Robert Blatchford launched his *Clarion* newspaper, on sale for a penny. *Clarion* was to be a socialist newspaper, which Blatchford intended would 'use the simplest and best language at our command' to work towards goals which he set out as 'justice, reason and mercy'. The paper quickly built a loyal, and large, readership, but it also acted as a catalyst for a wider social movement, particularly in the north, of working-class people who went out on Sundays and holidays into the countryside to escape from their weekday confinement in grimy industrial towns and to debate the way forward to a better tomorrow.

There were Clarion walking groups and Clarion choirs. There were Clarion Players amateur dramatic groups. Most importantly there was the Clarion cycling club, established in Birmingham in 1894 in the earliest days of popular cycling. Clarion cycling groups spread rapidly across the country. Both women and men enthusiastically joined the cause, becoming in Blatchford's words 'travelling prophets of a new era'.

And to help provide informal meeting places for this new movement, there were Clarion clubhouses too. Manchester Clarion cyclists acquired the lease on a house near Knutsford, Cheshire, in 1897 which they used for 'refreshment, recreation and accommodation', before moving in 1903 to a second building in nearby Handforth. Yorkshire Clarion cyclists also established their own centre on the slopes of the Chevin near

Menston, building a clubhouse which can still be found today.

On the other side of the Pennines, the central Lancashire mill town of Nelson, within sight of Pendle Hill, had grown very fast in the second half of the nineteenth century thanks to the expansion of the cotton industry. With this growth had come an early reputation for radicalism. Nelson needed a Clarion House, too, and the first clubhouse was opened in 1899 in a tiny cottage about two miles (three kilometres) from Pendle Hill Big End. Initially about forty members were involved. As one of its founder members Andrew Smith put it many years later, 'Factory workers most of them, they sought fresh air and the green fields of the countryside during the short weekend period when the looms no longer held them captive.' The Clarion was a meeting place offering both refreshments and fellowship: 'It helped to unite members in a common cause, and a common purpose.'

The impetus behind the Clarion House was taken by the Nelson branch of the Independent Labour Party, an organization which had been brought into being at a national conference six years earlier (Keir Hardie was a leading member) and which later was to play a key role in the founding of the Labour Party. Nelson itself was to return one of the first Labour MPs to Parliament in 1902.

The first Clarion House turned out to be too small, and so did a second replacement building, which was opened a few years later. In 1912, therefore, the Nelson ILPers decided to buy a plot of land on Jinny Lane, between Newchurch-in-Pendle and Roughlee, and to construct there a purpose-built Clarion clubhouse.

Known as the Clarion House, it has been open ever since, through good times and bad. It was a meeting place for conscientious objectors during the First World War, an

The Clarion House near Pendle Hill

organizing centre during the 1926 General Strike, and a place where unemployed workers in the hard years of the 1930s could have a holiday break. In the Second World War, it provided a temporary home for a party of refugees fleeing from Nazi Germany. More recently, it provided the venue for a day out in the country for striking miners during the 1984–5 strike. The Clarion House has also had strong links over the years with ramblers' groups, including the local Pennine Paths Association which worked tirelessly to ensure that rights of way were kept open and unobstructed.

As in the early days, today the Clarion House is run by a voluntary committee, who mow the lawn, touch up the paintwork and get the water boiling every Sunday for whoever drops by. As the centre's publicity leaflet puts it, 'We offer a warm welcome to both seasoned walkers and families out for a Sunday stroll.'

And the leaflet sums up the Clarion House philosophy in the following succinct way: 'The Clarion is a simple stop off for those who find contentment from their own labours, the great outdoors and friendly company.'

WALK 12

DARWEN MOOR

DIFFICULTY 🥾🥾 **DISTANCE 6½ miles (10.5 km)**

RODDLESWORTH (TOCKHOLES) — JUBILEE TOWER — DARWEN MOOR — RODDLESWORTH

MAP OS Explorer 287, West Pennine Moors

STARTING POINT Roddlesworth countryside information centre near Tockholes (GR 665215)

PARKING Car park at the information centre

PUBLIC TRANSPORT Buses run from Blackburn and from Darwen during the week. There are very occasional buses from Blackburn on Saturday; buses run approximately every two hours from Blackburn and Bolton on Sunday. (Alternatively, the tower and Darwen Moors can be reached from Darwen itself.)

An enjoyable walk to Darwen's famous landmark, and on to the moorland behind it. Generally on paths and tracks, although a little rough walking.

▶ From the bus-turning circle at Roddlesworth, take the bridleway towards the hills. After about ½ mile (0.8 km), the track enters woods **1**. Shortly afterwards, turn left across a bridge over the stream and then immediately right, taking the footpath up the side of the hill. At the top, head towards Darwen Tower **2**.

■ Darwen Moor's distinctive landmark was built in 1897. Known as the Jubilee Tower,

133

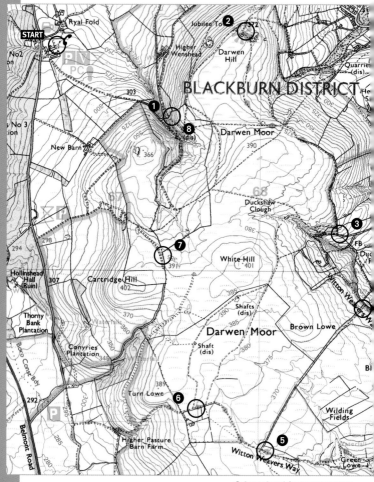

© Crown Copyright 100043293 2004

the tower was erected to commemorate the Diamond Jubilee of Queen Victoria, celebrated in June that year.

Or at least that's the official story. There was another reason behind the construction of the tower, and that was to celebrate the historic victory which local people had just won to secure open access to the moor. As an anonymous letter in the *Darwen News* proposing the tower put it, it was to be 'a landmark to be seen far and wide, and while commemorating the record year, it would also fulfil a similar function with regard to the celebration of the Freedom of the Darwen Moors'.

Darwen Moor had for centuries been well walked. In the later years of the nineteenth century, however, driven grouse shooting was developing and the local landowner, the Reverend Duckworth, wanted to keep Darwen Moor's grouse undisturbed for his own use. He began to block long-established routes across the moor, but was met by much opposition from local working people. Long years of arguments, prosecutions and direct action followed before, finally, the case went to the High Court. In 1897, Darwen people learned that nearly 300 acres of Darwen Moor were now, legally, theirs to enjoy.

The event was celebrated on 6 September 1896 in fine style, with a civic procession to the moor in which about 15,000 people were reported to have taken part. It was, ironically, the same day as that chosen in Bolton for a demonstration for access to Winter Hill (see pages 144–6).

The tower suffered from storm damage in 1947 and from subsequent vandalism, and its future was for a time in doubt. However it was restored and reopened in 1972. Currently the lower viewing platform is open, as are the stairs to the top of the tower; the top viewing platform is closed.

Darwen's pioneering place in Britain's access movement is not always remembered. However, a centenary celebration was held by walkers and others in 1996.

▶ Take the footpath which heads south across the moor from the Tower, following Witton Weavers waymarks. Continue on the Witton Weavers Way round the side of the moor, before dropping down to reach a tarmac lane ❸.

■ From the moors there are good views down to Darwen and beyond. Darwen's main landmark is the India Mill chimney, modelled by architect Ernest Bates on the bell tower in St Mark's Square, Venice. There is a – probably apocryphal – story that a celebratory dinner, complete with brass band, was held at the top of the chimney when it was completed.

The Peel Tower (Holcombe Tower) on the moors near Ramsbottom can also be seen, weather permitting, in the distance.

▶ Follow the tarmac lane briefly, over the bridge over the Duckshaw Brook. Beyond the bridge, as the road turns right, the Witton Weavers Way continues ahead, once more on the open moor. After a few hundred yards (metres) ❹, turn right off this path, along the footpath that runs south-west across the heart of the moor .

Although a right of way, this footpath is not easy walking, with plenty of grassy tussocks to contend with.

Eventually, the path meets a well-defined track. At this point ❺, it's possible to cross over and to explore the Hanging Stones and Big Grey Stones. From the Hanging Stones, a very faint sheep trod follows the line of the boundary wall north-eastwards: this is also very hard going, with tussocks galore to tackle.

Alternatively, for much easier walking, turn right on to the track (rejoining the route of the Witton Weavers Way). Follow the track for a short distance until you reach a gate ❻.

■ There is a signpost here, erected by the Peak District

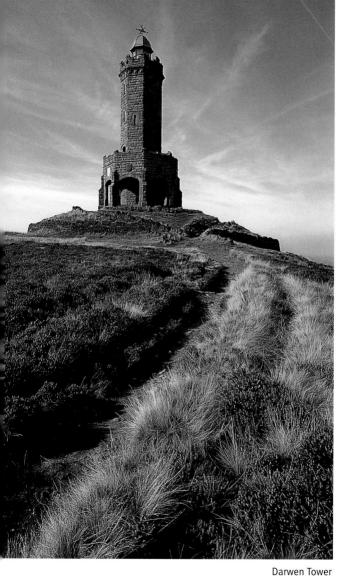

Darwen Tower

and Northern Counties Footpath Preservation Society (later the Peak and Northern Footpaths Society). This organization, formed in 1894, is the oldest surviving organization in Britain dedicated to defending walkers' rights.

▶ At the gate, turn almost back, to pick up the path running off to the right (signposted to Darwen).

After a short distance, when the main path turns to follow a fence, continue ahead, cross the fence at a hurdle stile and pick up a narrower track across the moor (not shown on OS maps.)

■ The path runs close to the site of an old mine shaft. Darwen Moor has a long industrial history, having been the scene of coal

mining for over 300 years. The coal was of relatively poor quality, but was used among other things to run local mill steam engines. Today the moor has the remains of many filled-in shafts and spoil heaps.

▶ Continue along the path as it bends round to the right, eventually arriving at a stile. Cross the stile but immediately turn right **7**, to contour along the side of Cartridge Hill (a fence is to the right).

When you meet a much more defined path, turn right, cross the stream at the bottom of the hill and almost immediately turn left. This is the path back down the side of Stepback Brook **8**, heading straight back to Roddlesworth and the starting point of the walk.

WALK 13

ROUND LOAF (ANGLEZARKE MOOR)

DIFFICULTY 👟 👟 **DISTANCE** 9 miles (14.5 km)

BELMONT WILL NARR LEAD MINES CLOUGH ROUD LOAF GREAT HILL REDMONDS EDGE WILL NARR BELMONT

MAP OS Explorer 287, West Pennine Moors

STARTING POINT Belmont village, on A675 between Bolton and M65

PARKING In Belmont. Alternatively, there is parking for about four cars at Hordern Stoops (Belmont–Rivington road), at GR 655158. (Starting the walk here saves about 2 miles/3 km in distance.)

PUBLIC TRANSPORT Buses from Blackburn and Bolton pass through Belmont.

A circuit of the heart of Anglezarke Moor, mainly on footpaths and tracks. The Bronze Age tumulus of Round Loaf and the viewpoint of Great Hill are the landmarks.

▶ From beside the Belmont Bull pub, take the footpath to the side of Hordern Pasture, making for Hordern Stoops ❶.

From Hordern Stoops follow the main path to Great Hill north for a very short way. Turn left on to an initially faint path just before the first high ground (Will Narr). This right of way, shown on maps, leads across the moor to the ruins of Higher Hempshaw's and Lower Hempshaw's.

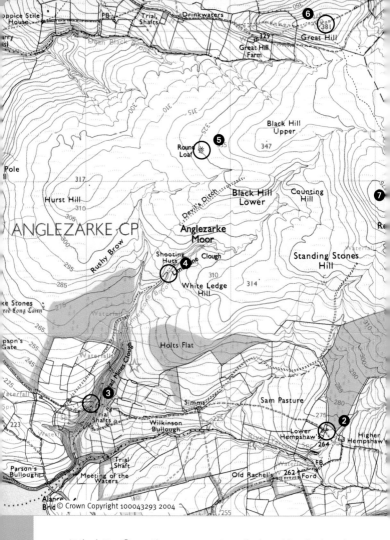

At the latter **2**, continue straight ahead (when a more defined track turns to the right) to walk alongside a broken-down field wall. (Officially the right of way keeps the wall to its left; it is

probably easier to continue with
the wall to your right.) At the end
of the field, the path becomes

more visible, continuing across
the rough ground of Sam Pasture.
Follow the path (it can be wet

underfoot) down to a stream and up to the site of the former Simms Farm.

Beyond the Peak and Northern Footpaths Society signpost at Simms, the path meets a well-constructed moorland track. Turn left, and follow the track down to the bridge at Lead Mine Clough.

■ This area of Anglezarke moor was the centre of a lead industry for centuries, with mining possibly beginning as early as Roman times and continuing until the nineteenth century. A helpful interpretation board beside the bridge offers more information.

▶ Cross the bridge, and take the path which climbs up the hillside to the Wellington bomber memorial, above the clough ❸.

■ The memorial is to the crew of a Wellington bomber which crashed on the moors in November 1943. The plane was on a training exercise from a base in Leicestershire. The actual site of the crash was about a mile (1.6 km)

north of the memorial, on Hurst Hill.

From the memorial, there are views across to the Pigeon Tower and Rivington Pike, both visited in Walk 14.

▶ Take the path beyond the memorial, through bracken. When the path meets a track, turn right and follow the track until it ends, beside the waters of Lead Mine Clough. Now take the path which continues up the side of the main clough, with the stream to your right. This is a pleasant stretch of walking.

After a few hundred yards (metres) ❹, a well-defined path (not shown on OS maps) continues straight ahead uphill, leaving the side of the stream (another path continues to the right, alongside the water). Climb the hill, to emerge on to the open ground of Anglezarke Moor. Over to the right, the impressive mound of Round Loaf comes into sight.

Follow the path across the peat until you reach Round Loaf ❺.

■ Round Loaf makes a striking sight, particularly

when approached from the south. It is artificial and is assumed to have been constructed as a burial site in Bronze Age times approximately 3500 years ago. Round barrows such as Round Loaf were a feature of Bronze Age Britain, but this is a particularly large construction, the largest one of its kind in the north-west. It has yet to be excavated.

There are other prehistoric sites on Anglezarke Moor, as well as on Winter Hill to the south. To the south-west, Pike Stones is believed to have been a stone-and-turf-covered mound, subsequently levelled. Just to the south of Round Loaf runs an earthwork known as Devil's Ditch, which is also thought to date back to Bronze Age or late Stone Age (neolithic) times. The ditch is straight and serves no obvious purpose; it could conceivably have been created as a land boundary.

▶ From Round Loaf, the next target is Great Hill, a short distance away to the north-east.

The most straightforward route is to take the track heading almost due north, towards the trees growing beside Dean Black Brook. Cross the stream and turn right to find a way across to the main path up the side of Great Hill ❻.

■ Great Hill offers good views in all directions. Darwen Tower is prominent to the north-east, with – weather permitting – views extending towards Pendle Hill, Longridge Fell and the Bowland hills and even as far as Ingleborough. To the south, the Winter Hill television mast is, of course, the most prominent landmark.

▶ From Great Hill, take the recently flagged path south across the peat to Redmonds Edge ❼. Continue as the path drops down from Redmonds Edge and climbs up towards Spitlers Edge. At 1286 ft (392 m), this is the highest ground on Anglezarke Moor.

The path carries on beside a broken-down wall down from Spitlers Edge, climbing once more up to Will Narr. From here, follow the outward route back to the starting point.

The battle for Winter Hill

It was 6 September 1896, on the edge of the moorland south of Winter Hill. On one side of a moor gate were the police and the gamekeepers employed by the local squire Colonel Richard Henry Ainsworth; on the other, a demonstration of about 10,000 Bolton people, demanding the right to continue to use the track beyond to gain access to the hills. Not surprisingly, the police and gamekeepers gave way.

Bolton's 'mass trespass' for access preceded the 1932 events on Kinder Scout in the Peak District by more than thirty years, but has today nothing like the same resonance among ramblers. Indeed in Bolton itself the story was almost forgotten, until 1982 when a local historian and community activist Paul Salveson made the effort to research old newspaper articles and publications and produced his own excellent history of the 1896 events, *Will Yo' Come o' Sunday Mornin'?*.

The title of his booklet is taken from a verse composed immediately after the 1896 'battle for Winter Hill' by Teddy Ashton, the pen-name adopted by the local writer, novelist and dialect enthusiast Allen Clarke. The verse begins:

> *Will yo' come o' Sunday morning*
> *For a walk o'er Winter Hill?*
> *Ten thousand went last Sunday*
> *But there's room for thousands still!*
> *O the moors are rare and bonny*
> *An' the heather's sweet an' fine*
> *An' the road across the hill tops*
> *Is the public's – yours an' mine.*

The 1896 confrontation focused on Coalpit Lane, one of the main routes offering access to the moors from Bolton and the settlements near by. Colonel Ainsworth owned the local estate and was a keen sportsman who regularly shot grouse over his land. Almost certainly it was to defend his grouse shooting that in the summer of 1896 he decided to erect a gate across Coalpit Lane and put up 'Private' signs.

He was also politically very hostile to the radical currents sweeping Bolton and other northern towns at the time. It was one recently established grouping, the Bolton Socialist Party, who led the campaign to reopen Coalpit Lane. According to Paul Salveson, their demonstration initially attracted about 1000 people, but many more joined in as the march snaked its way from the settlement of Halliwell up Smithills Dean Road towards the moors. He quotes a report published a few days

The stone commemorating the 1896 Winter Hill demonstrations

later in the *Bolton Chronicle*: 'Amid the lusty shouting of the crowd the gate was attacked by powerful hands . . . short work was made of the wooden barrier, and with a ring of triumph the demonstrators rushed through onto the disputed territory.' From here, according to the *Chronicle*, the marchers crossed Winter Hill to the village of Belmont – and 'Thus ended a demonstration perhaps unprecedented in the history of Bolton.'

Two follow-up demonstrations took place in subsequent weeks, on Sunday 12 September, when thunder and lightning failed to dampen enthusiasm, and again on the following Saturday. But by this stage, Colonel Ainsworth had counter-attacked, issuing writs against many of the leaders of the protest. Six months later, in March 1897, ten people found themselves on trial at Manchester Chancery Court and – despite a host of defence witnesses testifying to the previous unhindered use of Coalpit Lane – the judgment went in favour of the landowner. Two defendants, Solomon Partington and William Hutchinson, found themselves facing costs of over £600.

Paul Salveson's retelling of the story directly inspired the organization of a commemorative march that year which followed the route taken by the 1896 demonstrators. Even in 1982, Coalpit Lane continued to be blocked by a gate with a sign saying 'Private Road, No Footpath'. But by 1996, when a second commemoration march was held, this time to mark the centenary, the local authority had been prevailed upon to step in and to formally declare the road a right of way.

The last verse of Teddy Ashton's song asks rhetorically:

> *Must poor folk stroll in cinders*
> *While the rich cop all the green?*

The answer, a century and more on, is that all can enjoy the beauty of Winter Hill, on Sunday mornings and every other time of the week.

WALK 14

WINTER HILL

DIFFICULTY 👢 👢 **DISTANCE 9 miles (14.5 km)**

BARROW BRIDGE — WALKER FOLD — SMITHILLS MOOR — WINTER HILL — NOON HILL — PIGEON TOWER — RIVINGTON PIKE — TWO LADS — BURNT EDGE — WALKER FOLD — BARROW BRIDGE

MAP OS Explorer 287, West Pennine Moors

STARTING POINT Barrow Bridge, to the north-west of Bolton

PARKING A visitors' car park is provided in Barrow Bridge (GR 687117).

PUBLIC TRANSPORT Bus 526 runs hourly from Bolton. The bus terminus is a very short distance from the starting point.

A tour of Winter Hill, including part of the route taken in 1896 during the access protests (see pages 144–6). Generally easy walking on paths and tracks, with one stretch of harder moorland walking.

▶ Walk westwards past the riverside cottages in Barrow Bridge, taking the footpath into the clough as the road turns sharp right to run up the hill. Climb the steps, and follow the field path leading to the settlement at Walker Fold. At the road ❶, turn right and walk a few yards (metres), to take the footpath that heads through Walker Fold Woods towards Sheep Cote Green Farm. Near Sheep Cote Green turn half-left, and continue on the path through a pleasant wooded clough until you emerge on to another tarmac road.

▶ page 150

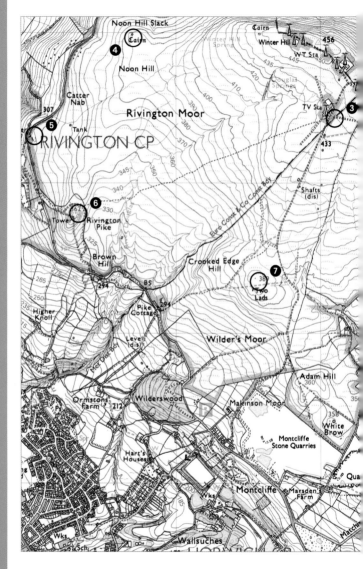

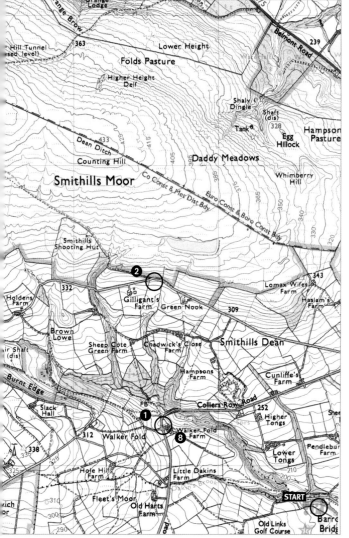

Grange Brow
Grange Lodge

Hill Tunnel
(used level)   363   Lower Height   239
                                                Belmont Road
                    Folds Pasture

                Higher Height
                Delf   Shaly
                                        Dingle
                                        Shaft   328
                                        (dis)
                        Tank   Egg   Hampson
                                        Hillock   Pasture

            433
Dean Ditch   415   Daddy Meadows
Counting Hill   405
                                                Whimberry
Smithills Moor   Co Const & Mex Dist Bdy   385   Hill
                                        365
                        Boro Const & Boro Const Bdy   350   340
                                                330   220

        Smithills
        Shooting Hut

                            2
Holdens   332   Lomax Wifes   343
Farm   Farm
                Gilligant's
                Farm   Green Nook   309   Haslam's
                                                    Farm
        Brown
        Lowe
            Sheep Cote   Chadwick's Close   Smithills Dean
        air Shaft   Green Farm   Farm
        (dis)   Hampsons
Burnt Edge   Farm   Cunliffe's
                                                Farm
        Slack   FB
        Hall   Colliers Row Road   252
                        1   Higher   She
            312   Walker Fold   Walker Fold   Tongs
    338   8   Farm
                                        Lower   Pendlebur
        Hole Hill   Tongs   Farm
        Farm   Little Dakins   210
                    Farm   200
    Fleet's Moor   Old Hants
    ich   Old Hants   START   Barr
    or   Farm   Old Links   Brid
            Golf Course

It's possible to cross into the open moors here. However, in order to commemorate Bolton's contribution to the story of countryside access in Britain, it's worth making a short detour along the road past Gilligant's Farm, to turn left through the gate into the moorland track known as Coalpit Road ❷.

■ This gate was the focus of the dramatic events in September 1896 when, for three weeks running, large demonstrations of local people took place demanding the right to continue to walk along Coalpit Lane.

Just beyond the gate, a stone commemorates the event. It was erected at the centenary celebrations, when Coalpit Lane was formally dedicated as a right of way.

▶ Coalpit Lane becomes a track across Smithills Moor. Near the television mast, follow signposts to the left to emerge almost directly under the mast ❸.

■ Winter Hill television transmitter was first

constructed in 1955–6 in time for the launch of ITV. The current mast, brought into service in 1966, is 1015 ft (309 m) high and consists of a 9-ft (3-m) high steel tube. A lift was built inside to give

access to the aerials.

A plaque on the side of the transmitter station records the Winter Hill air tragedy in November 1958, when a plane from the Isle of Man to Manchester crashed in poor visibility. Over thirty people died, though there were also seven survivors.

Another sad event, the murder of a young traveller called George Henderson on the moors in 1838, is

Rivington Pike

commemorated by a memorial pillar just beyond the television mast. This cast-iron pillar, known as Scotsman's Stump, replaced a tree which had originally been planted as a memorial.

▶ Follow the road as it bends round to the left, and continue walking past further telecom transmitters to the Winter Hill trig point.

■ Winter Hill is the highest ground in the West Pennine Moors, at 1496 ft (456 m).

▶ From here a path runs onwards, continuing along the crest of the hill. When it drops down towards the Rivington–Belmont road, make for the cairn on Noon Hill, a little away ahead and to the left ❹. With luck, you might find a sheep track to help; otherwise this next ½ mile (0.8 km) or so can be rough walking.

■ Noon Hill is the site of a prehistoric burial mound, excavated in 1958 by Bolton Archaeological Society. It was made of two circles of low stone walls, covered with earth, one about 33 ft (10 m) in diameter and one 52 ft (16 m) across.

Inside were found the cremated remains of two humans, and a broken urn. The urn was subsequently reconstructed and displayed in Bolton museum.

Noon Hill offers fine views across to the north towards Preston and Blackpool, and west and south to the Pigeon Tower and Rivington Pike.

▶ Drop down from Noon Hill to the track known as Belmont Road, and turn left to reach the Pigeon Tower ❺.

■ This striking folly marks the furthest extent of the fascinating Terraced Gardens built on the hillside up from Rivington by Lord Leverhulme. The son of a grocer, Lord Leverhulme was born William Lever and grew up in Bolton. He built his fortune initially through the success of Sunlight Soap, and demonstrated his philanthropic streak by constructing the model village Port Sunlight, in the Wirral. Lever's business developed into Lever Brothers, one of Britain's largest companies, and following a merger has now turned into the multinational Unilever.

Lever bought the Rivington estate in 1899–1900, and promptly set about commissioning the construction of the Terraced Gardens on the hillside above Rivington Hall. As well as the Pigeon Tower (built in 1910), this work included the elegant Japanese Gardens complete with pagodas, a landscaped waterfall, the Seven Arches stone bridge and a garden retreat, the Bungalow (now demolished). Lever later bequeathed Rivington Park, the Terraced Gardens and Rivington Pike to the people of Bolton.

After Lever's time the gardens suffered neglect, though recently they have at last begun to receive some of the attention they deserve.

▶ If there is time, it is worth strolling down into the Terraced Gardens from the Pigeon Tower.

The route of the walk continues along the unsealed road which leads from the Pigeon Tower straight to another well-known local landmark, Rivington Pike ❻.

■ Rivington Pike has been used on various occasions in history as a beacon site, including in 1588 when a beacon was lit to warn of the approach to British shores of the Spanish Armada. The squat tower dates back to 1733 when it was constructed on the orders of a local landowner, John Andrews, partly to confirm his ownership of the land after an expensive boundary dispute.

The Pike has been an important focus for local activity, and there is a long-established tradition of climbing it every Good Friday. A small fair is held at Easter, a relic of the much more significant Pike Fair which used to be organized here at Whitsun. In the nineteenth century, this seems to have been a lively and riotous affair, a contemporary newspaper report speaking of 'every species of debauchery' taking place during the Fair.

Rivington Pike is also the focus of a famous fell race, whose roots can be traced back to the late 1800s. The race in its modern form has been held continuously since the 1950s and involves a dash from Horwich to the Pike and back. By tradition, the Rivington Pike fell race is held on Easter Saturday.

▶ Drop down from the Pike to pick up the track heading south-east around Brown Hill. At Pike Cottage (which houses a 'Dog Hotel') turn left, to follow a footpath for one further short climb, back on to the moor, aiming for the high ground

known as Two Lads Hill (the name is omitted from OS maps, which shows only a spot height of 389 m) ❼.

■ Although allegedly marking the site where two children perished in a snow storm, the cairns at Two Lads Hill are actually on the site of what was probably another prehistoric burial mound.

▶ Take the path which continues beyond Two Lads Hill, following it until it eventually meets the Winter Hill tarmacked approach road. Cross this, and take the more northerly of the two signposted paths (to Walker Fold). After a short time, follow the path round to the right and climb on to the top of the outlying hill, Burnt Edge. From here make your way by footpaths back to Walker Fold ❽, from there retracing your steps to Barrow Bridge.

Some further reading

Here is a small selection of books which will tell you more about the Forest of Bowland, Pendle and West Pennines Moors areas. Please note that not all of these books are still in print.

Joe Bates, *Rambles Twixt Pendle and Holme,* 1920s

Walter Bennett, *The Pendle Witches,* Lancashire County Books, 1957 and 1993

Mike Cresswell, *West Pennine Walks,* Sigma Leisure, 1998

John Dixon, *Dunsop Bridge, Bowland Forest: Eight Family Walks,* Aussteiger Publications, 2003

John Dixon, *The Forest of Bowland,* Aussteiger Publications, 2004

Kenneth Fields, *Three Towers Challenge Walk,* Kenneth Fields, 1999

Kenneth Fields, *A Visitor's Guide to Rivington,* Kenneth Fields, 1998

Ron Freethy, *Exploring Bowland and the Hodder,* Countryside Publications, 1987

Philip Graystone, *Walking Roman Roads in Bowland,* Centre for North-West Regional Studies, University of Lancaster, 1992

M. Greenwood and C. Bolton, *Bolland Forest and Hodder Valley,* 1955; new edition Landy Publishing, 2000

Spencer T. Hall, *Pendle Hill and its Surroundings,* 1877; new edition Landy Publishing, 1995

Paul Hannon, *Bowland,* Hillside Publications, 1994

John Howard, *A Roman Road and its Culverts,* John Howard, 2002

Philip Hudson, *Coal Mining in Lunesdale,* Hudson History, 1998

Stan Iveson and Roger Brown, *Clarion House: a Monument to a Movement,* Independent Labour Publications, 1987

Jack Keighley, *Walks in Lancashire Witch Country,* Cicerone Books, new edition 2004

Jack Keighley, *Walks in the Forest of Bowland,* Cicerone Books, 1997

A.A. Lord, *Wandering in Bowland,* Westmorland Gazette, 1983

W.R. Mitchell, *Lost Village of Stocks-in-Bowland,* Castleberg, 1992

John Nickalls (ed.), *Journal of George Fox,* Religious Society of Friends, 1952 and 1975

Richard Peace, *Lancashire Curiosities,* Dovecote Press, 1997

Denis Pye, *Fellowship is Life: the National Clarion Cycling Club 1895–1995,* Clarion Publishing, 1995

John Roby, *Traditions of Lancashire,* 1829; reissued as *More Lancashire Myths and Legends vol 2 (More Legends of Lancashire),* Book Clearance Centre, 2002

Donald Rooksby, *And Sometime Upon the Hills (The Quakers in North-west England 3),* Donald Rooksby, 1998

Donald Rooksby, *The Man in Leather Breeches (The Quakers in North-west England 1),* Donald Rooksby, 1994

Paul Salveson, *Will Yo' Come O' Sunday Mornin'?,* 1982; new edition Transport Research and Information Network, 1996

P.L. Watson, *Rivington Pike, History and Fell Race,* Sunnydale Publishing, 2001

The Country Code

An abbreviated version of the Country Code, launched in 2004 and supported by a wide range of countryside organizations including the Ramblers' Association, is given below.

Be safe – plan ahead and follow signs

Even when going out locally, it's best to get the latest information about where and when you can go; for example, your rights to enter some areas of open land may be restricted while work is being carried out, for safety reasons or during breeding seasons. Follow advice and local signs, and be prepared for the unexpected.

Leave gates and property as you find them

Please respect the working life of the countryside, as our actions can affect rural livelihoods, the safety and welfare of animals and people, and the heritage that belongs to all of us.

Protect plants and animals, and take your litter home

We have a responsibility to protect the countryside now and for future generations, so make sure you don't harm animals, birds, plants or trees.

Keep dogs under control

The countryside is a great place to exercise dogs, but it's every owner's duty to make sure their dog is not a danger or nuisance to farm animals, wildlife or other people.

Consider other people

Showing consideration and respect for other people makes the countryside a pleasant environment for everyone, whether they are at home, at work or at leisure.

Index

Abbeystead estate
      19–20, 25, 42–3,
      55–8
access agreements
      21, 25, 45, 52
access campaigning
      17–20, 75–6, 132,
      133–6, 144–6,
      147, 150
access legislation
      8, 11–15, 34,
      42–3, 44–6
aircraft crashes 88,
      142, 151
Anglezarke Moor
      139, 142–3
Barley 121
Belmont 139
birdwatching 12, 15,
      36, 91–3
Bleadale 59, 65
Bleasdale 50,
      53–4
bogs 32–3
Bowland Area of
      Outstanding
      Natural Beauty
      16, 23
Bowland Knotts 108
Brennand 22, 71–3
Brennand Great Hill
      19, 71, 75–6
Brennand Tarn 76–7
Bronze Age 53–4,
      139, 143
Burn Fell 87–8
buses 66

centre of Britain,
      claimed 67–9, 73
Chipping 52
Clarion House
      129–32
Clitheroe 113
Clougha 21, 24–5,
      45, 55, 78
coal mining 22,
      100, 138
Countryside Agency
      15, 44
Countryside and
      Rights of Way Act
      see access
      legislation
Cross of Greet
      105, 110
crosses, medieval
      88–9, 90, 110
Darwen 133–7
Deep Clough 28
Deerstones 124, 128
Defoe, Daniel 10
dialect 37–8
dogs 12
Dunsop Bridge
      67–9, 71
English Heritage 15,
English Nature 15,
      32–3, 44, 91
excepted land 13–14
Fair Snape 45, 47, 52
fell running 52,
      116, 154
Fiendsdale Head
      33, 52

floods 97
Fox, George 28,
      111–12, 117
geology 22, 120
grading of walks 11
Great Hill
      (Anglezarke) 143
Greave Clough
      Head 40
Grizedale 34–6
grouse 12, 15, 17,
      20–21, 55–8, 135
Harrisend Fell 34–6
Harterbeck 98
Hawthornthwaite
      39–42, 55
Hayshaw Fell 35
Hazelhurst Fell 47
hen harriers 91–3
High Salter 90, 95
High Stephen's
      Head 27–8
Hodder, River 64
Hopkins, Gerard
      Manley 64–5
Hornby Road 78–82,
      88–90
Independent Labour
      Party (ILP)
      130–32
industrialisation 22,
      71, 138
Lancashire county
      council 21, 25, 42,
      44–6, 52
land ownership 17,
      45, 55

Langden Castle 52, 55, 65
lead mining 22, 64, 71, 142
Leverhulme, Lord 152–3
Littledale 30
Longridge 64, 143
MacColl, Ewan 7
Mallowdale 28, 55
'Manchester Rambler, The' (song) 7
Marshaw 42
Middle Wood centre 95–8
moorland management 32, 55–8
mountain and moorland rescue 10–11, 60–64
Ogden reservoirs 127
Outhwaite 100
Parlick 47, 52–3
peat 32–3, 42
Peel Tower (Holcombe) 136
Pendle Hill 16, 22–3, 64, 88, 111–12, 113–20, 121–8, 130, 143
Pendle Way 126
Pendle 'witches' 127–8
Pigeon Tower 142, 152–3

public transport 66
Quakers 28–30, 111–12, 17
Queen's Chair 25
Quernmore 22
Ramblers' Association 8, 76
Raven's Castle 101–4, 105, 109–10
restrictions on access 11–15
Rimmer, William 94
Rivington Pike 142, 152–4
Robin Hood's Well 117–18
Roby, John 101–4
Roeburndale 95–7
Romans 78–82, 142
Rothman, Benny 8, 76
Round Loaf 139, 142–3
RSPB 91, 93
Sabden 121–4, 128
Saddle Fell 45, 65
safety 9–11
shooting 14, 20–21, 55–8
Slaidburn 22, 71, 78, 80, 83–6, 90, 94
Slaidburn Silver Band 94
Smith, Chris 76
Stocks reservoir 105–7, 110

Tarnbrook 55
Totridge 33, 59, 64–5
trespassing 7–8
Trough of Bowland 70–71, 77
United Utilities 21, 55
Ward's Stone 24–7
waterfalls 99–100
West Pennine Moors 23
Westminster, Duke of see Abbeystead estate
Whin Fell 71
White Hill 19
White Moor 21, 45
Whitendale 83, 88–9
Whitendale Hanging Stones 68–9, 73
Whitewell 71
Winter Hill 143, 147, 150–52
Winter Hill, battle of 135, 144–6, 147, 150
Witton Weavers Way 136
Wolf Fell 45, 64
Wolfhole Crag 71, 73–4
Worston 113–15
Wray 97
Yorkshire, former county boundary 21, 70–71, 110

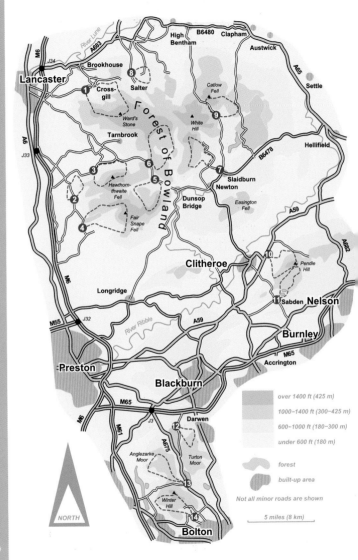